SHEFFIE
BEFORE
SHERLOCK

Peter Carter

SHEFFIELD BEFORE SHERLOCK

Some true cases of Victorian Crime Detection

PETER CARTER

Pages 4–5 and 116–117

Map of Sheffield, 1850–1863

This NEW PLAN of SHEFFIELD, is reduced from the large Ordnance Survey, *and comprises all the subsequent Improvements, new Streets, &c. from 1850 to 1863 as surveyed by J.Brigly, Esq. for the Publisher W.White, Collegate Crescent.*

Most of the reports referred to in the text were published in the two principal Sheffield newspapers, the *Independent* and the *Telegraph*. Occasionally, depending on the edition, there were minor title variations, but for simplicity, all these reports are cited at the end of each chapter under the following abbreviations:

Sheffield and Rotherham Independent (and its variants): SI

Sheffield Daily Telegraph (and its variants): SDT

Reports from the *Sheffield Daily News and Morning Advertiser* are referenced as SDN, while reports from other newspapers are cited under their full titles.

All Images © Peter Carter; except Pages 4-5, 23, 30, 34, 59, 80, 92 and 112-113 Picture Sheffield; page 20 © Chard Remains.

Published and printed by Arc Publishing and Print 166 Knowle Lane Sheffield S11 9SJ

Telephone 07809 172 872 email chris@arcbooks.co.uk www.sheffieldbooks.co.uk

CONTENTS

Two years ago, as part of a family history project, I investigated the lives and times of the Brayshaw family, who lived in the Wharfedale village of Harewood during the eighteenth and nineteenth centuries. Thomas and Hannah Brayshaw raised a large family. Most of their children took up employment, married, and settled locally; but their son Richard broke new ground: in 1851, he left his Harewood home and moved eighty miles south, to Sheffield – where he became a policeman.

I knew little about the work of the British police in Victorian times, except for the events that occurred in 1888, when London experienced a series of criminal atrocities, the "Whitechapel Murders". Despite all its efforts, the Metropolitan Police Force failed to arrest the person responsible ("Jack the Ripper") and so attracted many accusations of incompetence.

To make matters worse, a recently published detective novel was becoming very popular. Arthur Conan Doyle's *A Study in Scarlet* had introduced Sherlock Holmes – a character crafted with such skill and persuasion that the distinction between fact and fiction became blurred. Readers marvelled at Holmes's amazing powers and may have agreed with Doyle's unflattering portrayal of Scotland Yard's detectives. Some critics even suggested that this brilliant newcomer should be put in charge of finding the Ripper.

So, if Britain's detectives were considered inefficient in 1888, how effective would they have been during earlier decades? Did they form British policing's "dark age"?

As soon as I began to investigate Richard Brayshaw's career in the Sheffield Force, it became clear that anxieties about police efficiency could be dismissed. Richard became a senior member of Sheffield's hard-working team of detectives, and it was my good fortune to discover that regular reports of their work had appeared in the local newspapers. This book is based on a selection of the cases they solved, twenty years or more before Conan Doyle's great hero appeared on the scene.

In Sheffield, at least, there was no "dark age".

Peter Carter
Sheffield, May 2018

Sir Robert Peel MP (1788 – 1850)
This statue stands in front of the Town Hall at Tamworth, the
Staffordshire constituency Sir Robert represented for 20 years.

CHAPTER ONE

A FRESH START

During Britain's Industrial Revolution, Sheffield's population rose quickly, as people came into the town,[1] filling new jobs in its mining, steel, and cutlery industries. At that time, public services were provided by a diverse range of institutions, including the Town Trustees, the Church Burgesses, and the Company of Cutlers in Hallamshire. The task of maintaining law and order was handled by the town's Watch Committee, which supervised a team of watchmen and constables. These services had all operated well over the years since the time when Sheffield was a relatively small community. But as the town expanded and became increasingly industrialised, they were finding themselves overstretched. So, in 1818, following the example of many other growing towns across the country, Sheffield petitioned Parliament to grant powers that would allow public services to be harmonised and reorganised to meet modern requirements. In due course, the Sheffield Improvement Act was passed, creating the Borough of Sheffield and giving it these increased administrative powers.

The changes took several years to plan and implement.[2] While this work was underway, the *Sheffield and Rotherham Independent* expressed its approval:

The Cutlers' Company and the Town Trust, within their limited spheres, are useful organizations. They are good so far as they go. They sufficed when Sheffield had a population of 30,000 or 40,000. But with 100,000 inhabitants, with a town now spreading itself over many parts that used to be open countryside, an organization greater in power, more comprehensive in its range, and more popular in its character, is required. [3]

Modernisation of England's police forces was pioneered in London by the Home Secretary, Sir Robert Peel: the Metropolitan Police Force was established in 1829. Over the following years, many towns copied the Met's structure and procedures. [4] When Sheffield's Watch Committee was reorganised in 1843, its first duties included the appointment of a Chief Constable and, in 1844, the publication of *Rules, Orders and Regulations*, a document instructing members of the Sheffield Police Force in all matters concerning their duties and behaviour, which paid particular attention to Peel's fundamental principle:

It cannot be too forcibly impressed upon the minds of both officers and men, that the principal object to be obtained is "The prevention of crime."

To this end every effort of the Police is to be directed. The security of person and property, the preservation of the public tranquillity and of good order in the Borough, and all other objects of a Police Establishment, will thus be better achieved than by the detection and punishment of the offenders after they have succeeded in violating the laws. This should constantly be kept in mind by every member of the Police Force for his own conduct.

The absence of crime will be considered the best proof of the efficiency of the Police.

There was no mention of appointing officers who would specialise in crime detection; Watch Committee members firmly believed that "Prevention is better than Cure" – and perhaps they hoped that this approach would be sufficient. As things turned out, this proved not to be so, but the Watch Committee members would have been pleased to find their principle still alive in the 21st century. Today, though police officers no longer routinely patrol on foot, our streets and public places are commonly monitored by TV security cameras for evidence of suspicious or dangerous behaviour; and members of the public are actively encouraged and assisted by the police in protecting their property against theft and burglary.

At first sight, the Watch Committee's new strategy of crime prevention may have appeared simply to continue the historic use of town watchmen. But this illusion was denied by two prominent Sheffield citizens when they shared their reminiscences with a meeting of police officers and magistrates, many years after the changes had been introduced. [5]

Alderman William Smith recalled that:

There was a functionary called the parish constable, who was generally a small tradesman. When a crime was committed he put down his work, and put on his coat, and went to investigate the circumstances by himself. There was then no such thing as prevention of crime. Such was the state of things until 1839, when county authorities were empowered when they thought it proper to establish rural police. It has been a great blessing to the country, for it is infinitely better to prevent crime from being committed.

Sir Henry Watson described the appearance and practice of the night watchmen.

They carried rattles and long staffs, wore cumbersome great coats, and always sang out the condition of the weather and gave notice as to where they were: "Twelve o'clock, and a bright, moonlight night!" or "Twelve o'clock, and a wet night!"

That is not the principle of the present police force, whose aim is now to conceal their whereabouts and not let midnight marauders know where they are.

The 1844 *Rules, Orders and Regulations* made it clear that this new service was to be larger and more efficient: a team of police constables would patrol "beats" on foot, night and day, covering every street in the borough. The following paragraphs from this document indicate the Watch Committee's determination to be successful:

Every Officer and Police Constable should endeavour to distinguish himself by such vigilance and activity as may render it extremely difficult for anyone to commit a crime. He shall always appear neat and clean .... and be dressed in complete uniform, which shall be conspicuously marked and numbered corresponding with his name in the books, so that he can at all times be known to the public.

It is indispensably necessary that a patrolling constable should make himself perfectly acquainted with all the streets, thoroughfares, courts and houses on his beat.

If he observes anything likely to produce danger or public inconvenience, or which is irregular or offensive, he must report it to the supervising Sergeant.

He must visit every part of his beat as often as possible, walking at the rate of 2 ½ miles per hour, in order that any person requiring assistance, by remaining in one place for a short time may be able to meet with a Constable.

For centuries, it had been known that burglars, supposing that darkness reduced their chances of being caught, preferred to be active during night time. Two simple features of the new routine patrolling aimed to reduce the burglars' success rate:

When a constable goes on duty in the evening he is to see that all places are properly secured, and if any is found open, he is to inform the owner or occupier, if living near; but if the owner or occupier cannot be found, the constable must inform the Sergeant as soon as possible.

And to reduce the cover of darkness in the streets:

He will notice and report the state of the gas lamps, whether any are extinguished, dirty, or broken.

If burglary and theft could not be prevented by the patrols, the Watch Committee wanted officers to hold in their minds the possibility of catching offenders who were still in possession of their stolen goods.

If after sun-set or before sun-rising, an officer sees any suspicious person carrying a bundle or goods, which he suspects are stolen, he should stop and examine the person, and may detain him.

He must pay particular attention to such carts, and other vehicles, at night, as may be employed in conveying suspicious persons, or facilitating robberies.

Officers were also reminded of the cause-and-effect influence of too much alcohol.

An officer will pay particular attention to all public houses and beer houses in his beat, reporting to the Visiting Inspector or the Section Sergeant every instance of late hours or disorderly conduct.

To illustrate the system's thoroughness: in 1859, Sheffield's patrolling constables were deployed as two forces: [6]

A Day Force on duty from 6 a.m. to 9 p.m., having suitable hours allowed for rest and refreshment. During the day, the town was divided into 36 beats.

A Night Force on duty from 9 in the evening until 6 in the morning without any break. At night, the town was divided into 105 beats

However, Watch Committee members were realistic: they knew that a policy of prevention could not completely solve the problem of crime; patrolling constables had little chance of success when criminals

Old and New

In 1860s London, members of the public were helped to recognise a
police station by its display of a blue lamp. This became a tradition across
the whole country. Although less commonly seen in recent years, blue lamps
survive in some places, including the Woodseats Police Station in Sheffield.
Here it is accompanied by a security TV camera, a modern successor to
the patrolling police officer, observing activities on the nearby street.

waited out of sight and earshot before picking the lock, levering off the shutters or in some instances, thrusting the knife. So, in its *Rules, Orders and Regulations* the committee did not entirely concern itself with crime prevention; it also announced a rank of Detective Inspector – a man who would organise the officers' response, when a crime was reported. But at this early stage, no practical advice was given about lines of enquiry that officers might pursue. In the absence of such guidance, the earliest detective officers had to develop methods based on their own experience and judgement. In effect, they were left to get on with inventing detection. But, due to the emphasis on *prevention*, their numbers were small. In 1849, the Sheffield Police Force's payroll [7] revealed:

> 65 watchmen (retained until the previous system had been phased out) who were paid 14 or 15 shillings per week;
> 39 constables, paid at a higher rate: either 17 or 18 shillings per week;
> 1 "Detective Man" at 18 shillings per week;
> and 1 "Detective Man" who was paid an extra pound: he received £1,18 shillings per week.

Over the next ten years, the detective team gradually increased: in 1859, when the overall Force numbered 191, there were 156 constables, 1 detective sub-inspector, and 4 detective constables. [8]

But modest size didn't prevent the Sheffield detective team from achieving success; undeterred, it worked with enthusiasm and integrity; its members were resourceful, hard-working, brave, and intelligent. As their experience grew, powers of observation sharpened, and they acquired insights into the criminal mind. In some cases, the detectives would search for a thief, fully expecting this line of enquiry also to lead them to the stolen goods. On other occasions, when they reckoned that the stolen items would no longer be in the thieves' hands, investigations might be directed towards finding the receiver ("fence"). When money went missing, the police knew that it wouldn't have been stolen for investment; the thieves wouldn't be planning to open savings accounts in their local building societies. More probably, the money would be spent immediately. So, instead of searching for virtually unidentifiable coins and notes, detectives would be on the lookout for suspiciously large purchases or other changes in a criminal's life style.

Many of the crimes solved during these early years illustrate the Sheffield detectives' readiness to use the latest inventions. The country's railway network was growing rapidly, allowing people to travel faster and further than ever before. Unfortunately, this freedom was not restricted to law-abiding citizens; it was enjoyed by criminals, as well. They could now round off a night's thieving by escaping over the horizon to far-off safety, imagining that no-one could find them. But police officers travelled by rail, too; and also (unlike most criminals) used a more recent invention: electric telegraphy. Meanwhile, routine police work was undertaken by officers on foot or on horseback or, if working in a group, riding in a horse-drawn gig.[9]

At the police station, detectives kept log books, recording crimes (dates, names, addresses, descriptions of stolen items, etc.). Initially, these strengthened submissions of evidence in court; but detectives also found that by studying their accumulated records, they could identify some regular criminals' styles, and commit these to memory, for recall when a new crime was reported. Searches for suspected offenders were sometimes helped by advertising details in the *Police Gazette*, while other aids included the organisation of identity parades and, once it had become accurate and reliable, photography.

It would be disrespectful not to mention also that during this period, Sheffield's policemen were wisely guided and loyally supported by their Chief Constables: Thomas Raynor (1843-59) and John Jackson (1859-98).

Reflecting the restricted size of the detective team during these formative years, the cases described in the following chapters tend most often to involve a small group of officers: Ephraim Sills, Robert Airey, and Richard Brayshaw. But over the following years, extra funding allowed aspiring junior officers to be brought in, to increase the team's strength.

Footnotes

1. Although its population increased significantly during most of the nineteenth century, Sheffield remained a town until granted City status in 1893. On Tuesday, February 29, the *Sheffield Independent* printed Queen Victoria's pronouncement that Sheffield *"shall henceforth for the future and for ever hereafter be a CITY, and shall be called and styled 'THE CITY OF SHEFFIELD' instead of the Borough of Sheffield, and shall have all such ranks, liberties, privileges, and immunities as are incident to a City."*
2. This period is described by R.C. Mawby in his book *Policing Images* (Routledge, 2012)
3. 1843: SI, October 28.
4. Ahead of its launch, descriptions of the new Metropolitan Police Force appeared in local newspapers. For example, on 25 September 1829, full details were published in both the *London Morning Post*, and the *London Courier and Evening Gazette*. These were specially designed to suit London's size and complexity, but the document's introduction – *"It should be understood, at the outset, that the object to be attained is 'the prevention of crime'. To this great end every effort of the police is to be directed."* etc., was closely copied in 1844, when Sheffield's own *Rules, Orders and Regulations* were written.
5. 1887, SDT, 14 July.
6. 1859: SDT, 13 July; SDN, 14 July; SDT, 16 July.
7. 1849: SI, 3 November.
8. 1859, SDT, 13 July; SDN, 14 July; SDT, 16 July.
9. On Monday, 8 October 1860, when a prisoner escaped from the police station at Sheffield Town Hall, the *Sheffield Daily Telegraph* reported that in his pursuit, *"Officers were sent in every direction – some on horseback, others in gigs."* (A gig was a light, single horse, two-wheeled carriage, without a canopy.)

Court No.2 in the Old Town Hall, Sheffield

Many of the cases described in the following pages were heard in this 19th-century
courtroom. Sheffield's present Town Hall, overlooking Pinstone Street and the
Peace Gardens, was opened by Queen Victoria in 1897, but the old building on
Waingate (depicted on this book's back cover) continued to serve as a courthouse until
its closure in 1996. It now stands empty and, due to local road traffic management,
rather isolated. But its important role in the city's history has been recognised by
a Grade II listing; and a campaign to restore it as a valuable feature of Sheffield's
heritage has been spearheaded by the Friends of the Old Town Hall.

CHAPTER TWO

CAUGHT IN THE ACT

In 1837, when *Oliver Twist*, was published, readers could begin to enjoy Charles Dickens' tale of the Artful Dodger and his friends. But before then, Sheffield folk could read in their newspapers about pickpockets closer to home. For example, in 1828:

> *A man by the name of Turner who is employed on the Glossop Road, had his pocket picked of between twenty and thirty pounds on Tuesday last, between the Bank, where he had received them, and High Street. It is supposed the robbery was committed by some of the light-fingered gentry passing through this town to the races at Rotherham and Doncaster.*[10]

Patrolling police officers were on the lookout for pickpockets every day in Sheffield, mostly in crowded areas. When public events were held, at which large attendances were expected, the Chief Constable would arrange for extra officers to be present. The success of this strategy cannot easily be assessed, however, because crime prevention never hit the headlines. Newspaper readers weren't interested in events that didn't happen; but they evidently had a keen appetite for crimes that had been committed – and there were plenty of these. Many were handled by patrolling officers without needing help from the force's specialist detectives. But occasionally, detectives' involvement proved useful: through regular contact with the town's criminals, they acquired an extensive knowledge of habitual pickpockets[11] – and their favourite pubs.

※ ※ ※

One Saturday afternoon in February 1862, Detective Officer Robert Airey had called in to see Thomas Robinson, a watchmaker, in his Angel Street shop. While they were chatting, Airey happened to glance across the street, to the shops on the opposite side. There, he saw and recognised two men, James Higgins and James Smith. Both had records of conviction for pickpocketing, and they were now standing close behind two women whose attention was held by the goods displayed in a shop window. Airey strongly suspected what Higgins and Smith were up to, so he remained out of sight in Mr Robinson's shop, discreetly keeping the men under observation.

After a minute, one of the women walked away, but the other stayed there, as did Higgins and Smith until, after a quick glance up and down Angel Street, they ran off together up Hartshead, the nearby side street. Airey immediately left Mr Robinson's shop, ran across to the woman still at the shop window, and asked if she would check her pockets. When she did so, she discovered that all her money had disappeared. Though Officer Airey chased after Higgins and Smith up Hartshead, he failed to find them. But the following Tuesday evening, he found both of these men drinking at the *Beeswing* and charged them with the robbery.

In the magistrates' court, Mr. Robinson identified Higgins and Smith as the men he and Officer Airey had been watching from within his shop, and Mrs. Eliza Booth confirmed that she was the person who had been robbed. Both men denied having been in Angel Street at any time on Saturday but in view of the evidence, the magistrates were satisfied that Higgins and Smith had been "working" Angel Street. [12]

Sheffield's Victoria Railway Station and Hotel

The station opened in 1851, with the hotel following a few years later.
They are shown here as they would have appeared during the 1870s.
The station closed in 1970 but the hotel remains open.

⊗ ⊗ ⊗

Most pickpockets found their victims by roaming through crowded
town centre streets. But as the popularity of travelling by train
increased, railway stations became common haunts for criminals,
too. As far back as 1846, the *Sheffield and Rotherham Independent* had
published some words of advice:

> *Travellers by railway are cautioned to be strictly on their guard, since a
> number of robberies have lately been committed on the Midland stations.
> ..... There is little doubt that the crowding at the terminus during
> throng occasions, offers great facilities for pocket-picking.* [13]

The Sheffield police force included the town's railway stations in its schedule for crime-prevention patrols, but the following incident suggested that this task was becoming more demanding.

※ ※ ※

One evening in February 1859, a prominent local citizen, Major Richard Fawkes, and his wife returned by train to Sheffield's Victoria Railway Station. While they were making their way through the crowded exit towards a waiting cab, Mrs Fawkes felt someone press against her side. She then discovered that her purse was missing, and hurried to tell her husband, who had gone ahead to load their luggage into a cab. Mrs Fawkes pointed out a man who had been close to her when the theft had occurred – but he was now leaving the station's forecourt. So, Major Fawkes set off after him, and a passer-by came to his aid. Together, they stopped the man and challenged him to agree to be searched. They reassured him that if they found no stolen property on him, he would be proved innocent and allowed to continue on his way. At first, the man consented, but then he suddenly raced off down the road. Major Fawkes resumed his chase, shouting "Stop, thief!", and with the help of yet another passer-by, took the man, Joseph Haydon, to the police station at the Town Hall, where he was properly searched. But this proved negative: they found no trace of the purse.

Detective Officer Richard Brayshaw happened to be at the police station when Haydon was brought in – and recognised him: he had spotted him recently in the company of some notorious thieves in a local pub, *The Barrel*. Despite the unsuccessful search of Haydon's pockets, Brayshaw suggested returning to the road near the railway station, to re-examine the area where Haydon had been captured. In the darkness, they found Mrs Fawkes' purse – still lying where Haydon had discarded it, as he ran away. In court, Haydon admitted his guilt (and possibly regretted his choice of victim).

In court also, Major Fawkes addressed the magistrates. He

expressed his firm view that it was "improper" for Sheffield Victoria, unlike railway stations in other towns and cities he regularly visited, to have no railway police in attendance. The magistrates agreed, as did the Chief Constable – although he pointed out that this post would have to be funded by the railway company. [14]

Some railway police were eventually appointed; but a year later, the Victoria Railway Station was again the scene of a pickpocketing attempt, one evening when Detective Officers Airey and Brayshaw happened to be on duty. Their attention was drawn towards a man, later identified as Richard Hissot, who was working his way through the crowd that had poured onto the platform after the arrival of a train from Hull. Hissot moved in very close to a lady passenger and was then seen putting his hand in her coat pocket. The detectives duly apprehended him and took him into custody. The news reporter's account of Hissot's court appearance reveals a criminal secret (and possibly also the reporter's weariness):

Hissot had adopted the old but ingenious dodge of cutting a hole through the bottom of his coat pocket, with a matching hole in the outer fabric, so he could carry out his thieving while at the same time appearing to have his hand in his own pocket. When asked to account for being at the railway station, Hissot said he had gone there to meet a friend – who lived "nowhere", and also stated that he himself came from the same extraordinary place. [15]

At about four o'clock one morning during May 1859, Constable Charles Osborne was patrolling his beat along Granville Street, when a crime was committed, almost in front of him. A gang of three youths had broken into a local shop owned by Henry Glossop, a provision dealer, where they had stolen some cash and several items of food. Now, in the early morning light, they were running away along Granville Street, in full view of the constable and some groups of men walking to work, to start their early morning shifts. Any hope the youths may have had of escaping suspicion was spoilt by the fact that, although they had stuffed the cash and some small items in their pockets, they were very obviously carrying a 14kg cheese, and a 9kg ham shank. Shortly afterwards, two of the youths were apprehended and identified (quite easily in the case of the one whose home was on Granville Street) and the third was detained later. [16]

On a wintry evening in January 1862, while Sergeant Dyson Whiteley was patrolling along Union Lane, his alertness led to the discovery and interruption of a crime. At just before eleven o'clock, he spotted a moving light in an upstairs room within the premises of the cabinet makers, Messrs J W Peat. Suspecting that he could soon find himself dealing with an intruder, Sergeant Whiteley summoned assistance from his colleague on a neighbouring beat, police constable Joseph Cooper, and together they began to search the premises. In one of the rooms, they found Edward Henry Charlesworth, (a former employee of the firm). He had collected together several surgical instrument cases, a microscope and case, and some valuable tools, and packed them into a box, ready for removal. In court, Charlesworth pleaded guilty to a charge of attempted burglary. [17]

On Sunday evening, 18 December 1859, a week before Christmas, farmer Francis White checked that the seven geese he was keeping in his fold yard were all safe and secure. But the following morning, the yard was empty and there were blood stains in the adjoining shed. Mr White reported to the police that all his geese had been stolen.

By chance, at between five and six o'clock on that Monday morning, Detective Officers Richard Brayshaw and Robert Airey were on duty in the Park Hill area of Sheffield. While patrolling along a footpath leading from Blast Lane to Cricket Inn Road, they saw three men, about a hundred yards away, each carrying a sack over his shoulder. As the detectives drew nearer, the men set off running. Two dropped their sacks and ran ahead along the footpath, pursued by Brayshaw, while the third turned off in the direction of a brick kiln, pursued by Airey. This third man threw away his sack as he ran around the brick kiln and then headed back to the path where, in the darkness, he collided with Brayshaw. They both fell to the ground and a scuffle developed, which continued until Airey arrived, and the man was secured. He was identified as William Bywater, otherwise known as "Barrow Bill"[18], a man with a criminal record of fowl theft.

When cautioned, Bywater protested his innocence. He claimed that he had been at home all night and when detained was simply on his way to look for work. In any case, he denied that he had been carrying a sack. Bywater's sack was actually found to contain three dead geese, and the sacks abandoned by his accomplices each contained two dead geese. Shortly afterwards, Mr. White identified these seven birds as his stolen property.

In court, the jury dismissed Bywater's claims of innocence, and neither were they persuaded by his attorney's argument that geese cannot be identified by their colour, because all geese are either grey or white.

The Chairman of the magistrates' bench, addressing Detective Officers Brayshaw and Airey, said they had behaved very courageously, and had displayed great skill in capturing the prisoner. The magistrates directed that a reward of £1 should be paid to each of them. [19]

Herbert Birks, a Sheffield grocer and tea dealer with a shop in West Bar, had an 18-year-old assistant, Charles Morgan. After having employed him for about six months, Mr Birks began to have doubts about his assistant's honesty. He had found a notebook in which young Charles was keeping a record of his expenses. The figures showed that the amount of money he was spending was much greater than his wages. Mr Birks suspected that Charles Morgan had been supplementing his lifestyle with help from the shop's till. So, he contacted the Chief Constable.

Detective Officer Richard Brayshaw was delegated to visit Mr Birks. After assessing the situation, the officer proposed a scheme to Mr Birks, which (if he was willing to try it) would require help from some of his regular customers. He was to mark several coins with scratches or stains, then distribute the coins among his friends, asking that they should use them to purchase items from his shop, early the next morning. It was certain that they would be served by Charles Morgan because Mr Birks planned to arrive at the shop later than usual, perhaps about an hour after opening time. He would then send his assistant out on an errand, to keep him away from the shop for a while.

While Charles was away, Mr Birks checked the cash in the till, where he found all the marked coins, except for one half-crown. He reported this to Detective Officer Brayshaw, who then came to the shop and asked Charles Morgan to empty his pockets. Out came the marked half-crown and five pounds' worth of gold coins. Morgan then admitted his guilt. [20]

※ ※ ※

The counterfeiting of coins and bank notes was strongly linked to the crime of attempting to use these fakes as payment for goods or services. This second crime – the fraudulent use of money knowing it to be counterfeit – was termed uttering. The social and economic harm it caused was regarded as being equal to the effects of receiving stolen goods following a theft.

Counterfeit coins were produced by a two-stage process. Plaster moulds created from genuine coins, were used to cast coins made of base metal. These coins were then electroplated with silver. Sometimes the counterfeits were almost perfect reproductions (Sheffield being home to workmen skilled in the lawful use of these processes). But any minor scratches on the original coin's surface, as well as the date year, would appear identically on all the copies – and these repeated features could betray the coins as fakes.

Forgers worked secretly behind closed doors, presenting a great difficulty for the police officers given the task of discovering them. Success in finding "coiners' dens" could often depend entirely on information received from members of the public. And there was another problem: even with only a minute's notice of the police's arrival, coiners could quickly destroy their tools and their forgeries, leaving officers unable to gather evidence for presentation in court. So, as well as relying on tip-offs, the police needed speed and surprise for catching coiners "in the act".

※ ※ ※

In July 1861, Detective Officers Robert Airey and Richard Brayshaw paid a surprise visit to the home of Caroline and John Brown (alias Arthur Irwin). [21] The following extracts from Airey's verbatim evidence in court best describe what happened:

> *On Tuesday morning, between nine and ten o'clock, in consequence of some information I received, Detective Officer Brayshaw and I went to a house in Club Mill Yard. … When we started searching the house, I found a counterfeit sixpence that was still unplated. … Looking into the oven, I saw a pair of plaster of Paris moulds. Irwin rushed at me and Caroline Brown struck at me with a poker. … While we were putting the handcuffs on Irwin, he shouted to Brown "Break the moulds, break the moulds!" She did so, by kicking them with her feet. I picked up the pieces and we brought them to the Town Hall, where we put them together to make nearly a perfect pair of moulds. The unplated sixpence I found fits the moulds exactly.* [22]

For many years and in many ways, Sheffield and Leeds have been keen rivals; compliments are rarely exchanged. So, on 30 July 1862, readers of the *Leeds Mercury* may have been surprised to find "Clever Capture of Coiners in Sheffield" headlining the report of a recent case dealt with by the Sheffield Police Force.

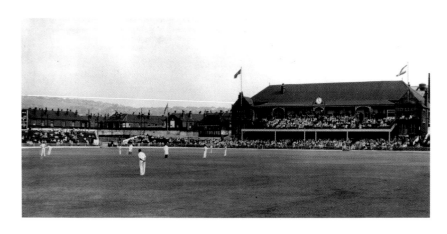

Cricket at Bramall Lane, Sheffield

Created as a cricket ground in 1855, Bramall Lane then, for over 100 years,
staged both cricket and football matches. But since 1973, it has
exclusively been Sheffield United Football Club's home ground.

Three Sheffield detective officers, Robert Airey, Richard Brayshaw
and William Leonard, were deployed to investigate two notorious
criminals, William Fieldsend and Thomas Oscroft, in their house,
described as "situated within its own garden on Bramall Lane, opposite
the cricket ground"[23]. A surrounding garden usually made it difficult
for police officers to approach without attracting the attention of the
people inside the house – but on this occasion, they managed it with
success. Airey and Leonard burst in through the front door and caught
the coiners busily engaged in their work. Meanwhile, Brayshaw had
taken up a position round the back of the house, ready to catch anyone
trying to leave by that route. Oscroft started to make an escape attempt
but changed his mind, when he caught sight of the waiting detective.
The coiners, all their equipment and a large number of counterfeit
coins were seized.

This was a major case, eventually tried at the York Assizes, where the judge's closing remarks put counterfeiting into its social context. Mr Justice Keating expressed his view that the evidence against these prisoners was of the clearest possible character, and that their crime was of a most dangerous nature because it led to a vast amount of fraud upon small tradesmen and others who could ill afford the loss. [24]

Footnotes

10. 1828, SI, September 13.

11. "Habitual" was an official term, used to describe criminals who had committed more than one offence. The *1869 Habitual Criminals Act* resulted in the establishment of a system for centrally recording details of criminals and ensuring better supervision. (For more information, see http://vcp.e2bn.org/justice/page11571-habitual-criminals.html)

12. 1862: SI, February 6, 10 and 15; SDT, February 6 and 10.

13. 1846: SI, August 15.

14. 1859: SDN, February 11; SDT, February 12.

15. 1860: SDT, February 16.

16. 1862: SDT, January 18 and 30; SI, January 29 and 30, and February 1.

17. 1859: SDT, May 13, 14, 18 and 23; SDN, May 13, 16, 19 and 21; SI, May 14.

18. Many criminals seemed proud to be known by a nickname. During 1860, Thomas Gordon, a Sheffield clothes thief apprehended by Detective Brayshaw, *[SDT: August 14]* seemed untroubled by being referred to as "Tailor Tom"; Richard Allen, a thief who roamed the West Riding for many years, was widely known as "Devil Dick" *[SI, September 15]*; and "notorious" William Grist operated as "Billy Gristle" *[SDT, June 18]*. Presumably, William Bywater often carried away his stolen items in a barrow.

19. 1862: SI, January 30; February 1, 3, and 8; March 4 and 8.

20. 1859: SDN, December 19; SDT, December 20 and 22; *Derbyshire Times*, December 24; SI, December 24, and 1860: January 14.

21. Although both suggest an involvement in crime, a distinction can be drawn between obvious and sometimes amusing nicknames (such as "Barrow Bill") and credible alternative names, such as John Brown / Arthur Irwin, which criminals deliberately use to evade identification.

22. 1861: SDT, July 4; SI, July 6.

23. Sheffield's Bramall Lane stadium is credited as being the oldest in the world still hosting professional football matches. (www.stadiumguide.com). But it opened on 30 April 1855 as a cricket ground and was used only for this purpose for the next seven years.

    The first football played at Bramall Lane was a charity match on 29 December 1862, between teams representing Sheffield and Hallam. Advertised over several days in the *Sheffield and Rotherham Independent*, the match's aim was to generate contributions to the *Lancashire Relief Fund*. This had been created to provide temporary financial help for the county's cotton mill workers, whose livelihoods were threatened when America's Civil War cut off their transatlantic supply of raw materials.

    Both football and cricket were played on the Bramall Lane pitch until 1973, when Yorkshire County Cricket Club played their last match there.

24. 1862, SI, July 29, August 2, and December 12; *Leeds Mercury*, July 30.

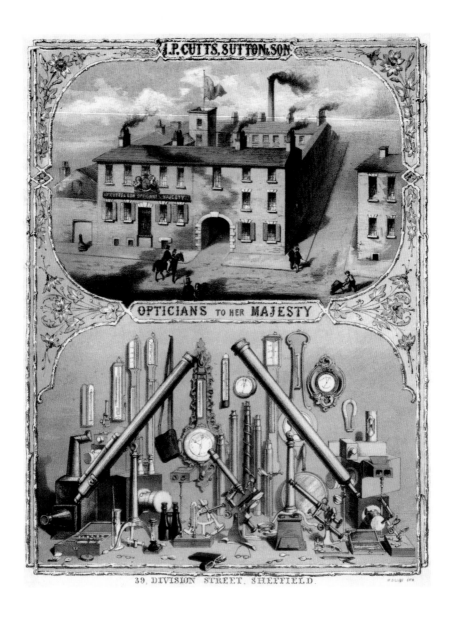

J.P. Cutts, Sutton & Son, Division Street, Sheffield.

This firm was among the many Sheffield manufacturers awarded royal patronage in recognition of their excellence. Unfortunately, the high quality of their products also sometimes encouraged night-time visits from local thieves and burglars.

CHAPTER THREE

FOUND IN POSSESSION

Some thieves chose to steal money rather than goods, believing they would be safe from detection, because all pennies look alike, and all shillings look alike, etc. But occasionally, they could be wrong.

※ ※ ※

Just before six o'clock on the morning of 4 November 1859, detective officers Richard Brayshaw and Robert Airey were on duty in Silver Street, when their attention was drawn to two men who were behaving strangely. The officers followed them, and their suspicions grew stronger when the men, now realising they were being followed, started running away. Although the men parted and ran off in different directions, the officers caught them and took them to the central police station at the Town Hall.

Very shortly after this incident, Francis Hill, an ironmonger, who lived above his shop in nearby Beet Street, woke up to find that burglars had stolen all the money from his till. He immediately set off to report his loss to the police.

At the police station, the two men detained on Silver Street were asked to explain why they were on the streets at that early hour. They were still being questioned, when the report of Mr Hill's burglary arrived – including the information that three of the stolen coins were marked in a distinctive manner: a fourpenny piece had two holes in it, one of the shillings had a star stamped on it, and a threepenny piece had a hole in it.

The detained men were asked to empty their pockets. Among the coins in their possession were a fourpenny piece with two holes in it; a shilling stamped with a star, and a threepenny piece with a hole in it. The detectives' suspicions were confirmed. [25]

Between four and five o'clock, one Saturday afternoon in April 1860, George Damms, the station master at Brightside railway station, received a message which called him away from the station for about twenty minutes. No other staff were on duty at the time, so before leaving, Mr Damms locked his cash box and put it securely in the booking office, which he also locked. The box contained about eleven shillings in silver, five shillings in copper, and 200 unused train tickets.

While Mr Damms was away, a local man, George Beckett, broke into the booking office and stole the box. He then took it to a secluded area near the railway track and forced it open, unaware that he was being watched by two keen-eyed schoolboys. Beckett pocketed the cash, abandoned the box, and then made his way to the nearby *Pheasant Inn*. There, to reduce the weight in his pocket, he talked the barmaid into changing three shillings' worth of his copper coins into smaller, lighter, silver coins. But he failed to notice that one of the pennies he handed over had a hole in it.

Meanwhile, Mr Damms had returned to the station and discovered the robbery. To his relief, the boys brought him the retrieved box – but it now only contained the train tickets. So, Mr Damms contacted the police. They took statements from the boys, then visited the *Pheasant*, where they were told about Beckett's recent visit. Mr Damms had already told them about the damaged penny, which the detectives now found among the copper coins in the pub's till. In court, Beckett claimed to have been nowhere near the railway station – but to no avail. [26]

One week during November 1862, Sheffield's Midland Railway goods warehouse received a consignment of newly-minted copper coins from the Soho Foundry Mint in Birmingham. The coins were securely packed in ten wooden boxes, strapped around with iron, and properly stored in the warehouse which was securely locked up by the foreman, Alexander Hill, on Saturday afternoon, at the end of the week.

The following Monday at about three o'clock in the morning, Mr Hill was urgently summoned to the railway station. The warehouse doors had been forced open and some of the Mint's wooden boxes had been broken open and scattered around. Nearby, lay a chisel, stolen the previous day from one of the station's stonemasons. About twenty packages, each containing sixty halfpenny coins, were missing.

Detective officer Brayshaw was called in to investigate. Joseph Shores, a labourer at the station, told him that one of the porters, Joseph Dunn, had been caught loitering near the main warehouse door on Saturday morning, at a time when he was supposed to be off duty, and should not have been allowed on the premises.

Detective Brayshaw's enquiries revealed that on the Saturday evening, Dunn had been out on a buying spree. He had bought a new hat from George Hewlett's shop on Snig Hill; redeemed a silk handkerchief from Dickinson and Eaton's, the pawn brokers, also on Snig Hill; and he had paid off a debt at Peel's, the tailors on West Bar. In each case, Dunn had paid with new halfpennies wrapped up in packages of 60. At Peel's, he had told the puzzled shop assistant that he was now employed at a firm where they often paid their employees in new coins. Dunn had then visited Messrs Beal's shop in King Street, where he handed over 240 new halfpennies in return for a decorative breast pin.

Detective Brayshaw, assisted by William Symons, a detective employed by the Midland Railway, apprehended Dunn at the railway station. They then took him back to his lodgings, where they found all his recent purchases and some surplus halfpennies. These were presented as evidence in court, where witnesses confirmed all Saturday evening's peculiar transactions.[27]

The premises of Messrs J P Cutts, Sutton and Sons, manufacturers of high-class optical equipment, stood on Division Street. Late one Saturday evening in September 1865, Thomas Dawson, who lived on Division Street, opposite Messrs Cutts' warehouse, spotted a flickering light in one of the upper storey rooms. Not sure whether this indicated that staff were working overtime or that burglars had broken in, he went to ask advice from a friend, Mrs Jane Sutton, widow of John Sutton, formerly a partner in the firm, who lived nearby. Mrs Sutton accompanied Mr Dawson back to Division Street where, after deciding that something suspicious must be happening, they contacted the police. Constables were summoned to surround the building, but their arrival alerted the burglars, who managed to escape. Two men, both carrying bundles, ran up Division Street but they then parted and took off in different directions. PC Joseph Bartholomew took chase and captured one of them, James Whiteley, a known thief, recently released from prison.

At the Town Hall police station, Whiteley's bundle was found to contain a large collection of expensive, high-quality opera glasses. Enquiries were placed in the hands of Detective Inspector James Rodgers, an experienced officer who knew Whiteley, knew that his associates included George Colton – who had also just served a prison sentence for robbery – and also knew Colton's address. So, accompanied by a constable, he went to Colton's house on Jessop Lane, where they found the other very valuable bundle.

Inspector Rodgers' investigations revealed that Colton had, by devious means, obtained a duplicate key to the back door of the warehouse. A further search of the premises uncovered a basket containing another large collection of optical instruments, which were to be picked up by the burglars during a return visit to the warehouse on Sunday, when the premises would be closed and unoccupied.

After checking the warehouse inventories, the proprietors were relieved to find within the burglars' bundles and the abandoned basket, all the items (including 200 pairs of spectacles) on their inventory of goods stolen from the warehouse. Whiteley and Colton were tried at the Leeds Assizes, where they both pleaded guilty. [28]

❈ ❈ ❈

During the working day, people employed in factories, shops or warehouses could sometimes feel tempted to steal from the stock around them. Experienced thieves knew that the sooner they disposed of their stolen goods, the better; if a policeman came to call and found them still "in possession", they stood little chance of escaping punishment. Inexperienced thieves, however, were often unaware of this obvious precaution, and the police – who knew that stolen items didn't simply disappear into thin air – also generally knew where to look for them.

❈ ❈ ❈

During the summer of 1862, Thomas Hydes, was having some alterations made to his ironmonger's shop, in the Sheffield town centre. He assumed that the contractor's men carrying out this work would all be trustworthy. But after a while, when some stock items started to go missing, his opinion changed. In particular, he began to doubt the honesty of one of the workmen, Charles Swift. The temptation of being surrounded by valuable (and re-saleable) tools and other goods appeared to have become too hard for Swift to resist.

Mr Hydes had notified the police of his suspicions, and Detective Officer Robert Airey was sent to investigate. After making a few discreet

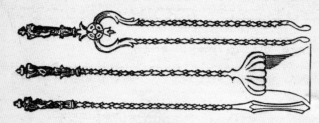

observations, Airey took up a position outside the shop's side door when work finished for the day, and detained Swift, as he was leaving. When searched, Swift was found to have a pair of shears, a pair of compasses, a lock and several other items of hardware in his possession. Accompanied by other officers, Airey then escorted Swift back to his home in Hanover Street, where they found a large number of tools, including over a hundred files, and other items of ironmongery. Swift had clearly been robbing the shop for some time. In court, he admitted his guilt. [29]

⊗ ⊗ ⊗

As well as having access to valuable manufactured items, employees could also be tempted to steal quantities of the raw materials used in Sheffield's cutlery and engineering industries. These materials could be sold on, via receivers, to unscrupulous manufacturers. Employers in industries where the staff handled gold and silver and other precious metals, had to be particularly careful, choosing only people who were honest and trustworthy.

⊗ ⊗ ⊗

John Wycliffe Wilson, the managing proprietor of the Sheffield Smelting Company, believed that his employee John Robinson was honest: he had worked for the company for many years without suspicion, smelting (heating up, refining and blending together) gold and silver. The materials he was given to treat with these processes included gold coins, usually those withdrawn from circulation through becoming too badly worn and defaced to function as currency.

But on 11 February 1863, some events occurred at the company's works, prompting Mr Wilson to communicate with the Chief Constable, who sent Inspector Robert Airey to investigate. At the works, the inspector searched Robinson, finding that he had in his pockets a sovereign, a half-sovereign, and about half an ounce of gold "paring" (gold mixed with silver). Robinson admitted that these coins were given to him to smelt, and that he had picked the paring off the workshop floor. He handed Inspector Airey the key to a drawer in his bedroom in which were later found eleven gold coins and nearly an ounce of fine gold. [30]

John Howell was employed as a blacksmith at the iron foundry of James Ellis and Co. He had been at the firm for about ten years and had always worked to Mr Ellis's satisfaction; but a rumour was now spreading that Howell had become a thief. To see if this could be true, Mr. Ellis paid a casual visit to Howell's workshop, where he noticed some pieces of iron lying around, which had no connection with the jobs in hand. His suspicions aroused, Mr Ellis contacted the police, and Detective-officer Brayshaw was sent to investigate.

After chatting to one of Mr Ellis's foremen, Brayshaw arranged a plan. At the end of the working day, he would take up a secluded position in the foundry yard, watching the employees as they left to go home. The foreman, standing near the foundry door, would give him an arranged signal to indicate which man was Howell.

So, Brayshaw detained Howell, took him into the firm's office and searched him. In his pockets, Howell was carrying ten iron rods cut into short lengths to make them easier for carrying, altogether weighing about 14 kg. Howell confessed his crime and told Mr Ellis he was sorry for what he had done. Afterwards, Brayshaw searched Howell's home in Matilda Street where, in the cellar, he found another 17 kg of stolen iron, intended for sale. Further enquiries revealed that Howell had been robbing the firm for about two years. In court, he pleaded guilty. [31]

※ ※ ※

Today, manufacturers of tableware use artificial, synthetic materials for handles, etc., but during the nineteenth century, before conservation became an ethical concern, natural materials, such as ivory, horn and shell were widely used.

※ ※ ※

William Wilde, a dealer in ivory, owned premises in Cambridge Street. One Tuesday evening in October 1861, he locked up his warehouse as usual, leaving it secure. Overnight, however, the warehouse was burgled. Pieces of ivory weighing altogether 64kg and hundreds of table and dessert knives and forks were stolen, along with 50 cigars and – apparently trivial but eventually significant – a reversible cloth overcoat.

The name of William Sellars, the keeper of a beer house, the *Bath Cottage* on Harmer Lane, was suggested to detectives Airey and Brayshaw. Two days after the theft, the officers paid a visit to the beer house and asked Sellars if he happened to be in possession of any property belonging to anyone but himself. Sellars replied that he was not. The detectives explained that even so, they must search the premises – prompting Sellars immediately to confess to possessing a handkerchief in which were wrapped some ivory-handled forks that could have been stolen items. Asked if he was in possession of more items, Sellars again claimed to be innocent. But he told the detectives that if they waited until nine o'clock that evening, a man named Jack Gardener would arrive at the beer house, bringing with him the remainder of the stolen cutlery.

The detectives recognised and dismissed this invitation as a crude delaying tactic, and promptly continued with their search. Upstairs, they found a young girl in bed. After refusing and protesting, Sellars eventually agreed to their request for the girl to get out of the bed. When she did so, the remainder of the stolen cutlery was revealed below the mattress. Airey and Brayshaw also found fifty cigars – and a reversible cloth overcoat. [32]

On Tuesday evening 28 October 1864, John Schofield, the manager of Messrs Francis Newton & Co., based in Sheffield's Portobello district, secured the outer door of the table knife warehouse as usual, with a lock bolt and a strong padlock, before going home.

But at about six o'clock the next morning, one of the factory's workmen, Joseph Deakin, roused Mr Schofield with some bad news: overnight, the factory had been burgled. The table-knife warehouse door, now bearing marks of a violent attack, was wide open; the engine-house door had been opened and someone had switched on the gas lights; a window frame had been broken, two bar fasteners had been removed; and the guard dog was missing. Inside the warehouse, a cupboard, in which there had been more than a thousand ivory handles, had been forced open and now stood empty.

The police were informed, and Detective Officer Richard Brayshaw was assigned to investigate. He collected evidence from various sources, that led him, three days later, to visit the warehouse of Messrs Jackson and Co. at Sheaf Island Works, Pond Hill. He arrived there during the mid-day break, and patiently waited until Ezra Garrett, of Hampton View, Walkley came in with a large bag on his shoulder. At Brayshaw's request, he opened the bag – to reveal the stolen ivory handles.

When charged in court with having committed the theft, Garrett (in the words of the newspaper reporter) "made the usual reply, that he had got them from a man he did not know, but he would know him if he saw him again". [33]

The restored Georgian splendour of Sheffield's Paradise Square gives little hint of its former appearance in the middle of the 19th century, when it was the location of John Heiffor's warehouse. Mr Heiffor ran a very successful company, founded by his father, Thomas, specialising in the manufacture of razors.

On the evening of 3 January 1861, the manager, James Hall, made sure the warehouse was securely locked; but during the night, it was burgled. Over a thousand razors, sixty razor cases, and nearly three hundred ivory inserts for razor handles were stolen. After large-scale warehouse burglaries such as this, the police almost routinely found that the thieves would afterwards tour around the local pubs and beer houses, trying to unload some of the stolen items.

A few days after the raid on Heiffor's warehouse, Charles Cocking entered the *Crown Inn* in New Street, via the back door, carrying a large sack full of paper parcels. With permission from the landlord, Bernard Sweeney, he placed the sack on a sofa and covered it with a rug, saying that he would be back in about half an hour. He duly returned, bringing some more paper parcels which he added to the pile on the sofa and again covered it over. All this activity was watched by the landlord's wife, Eliza Sweeney, and his serving maid, Eliza Flynn.

The following day, Detective Inspector Ephraim Sills and Detective Officer John Leonard came to the pub, making enquiries concerning the Heiffor's warehouse burglary. They found the sack and parcels and were told that they had been brought in and left there by Charles Cocking. The parcels were easily recognisable as having come from Heiffor's because they had all been signed by James Hall. As manager, it was Mr Hall's duty to check every item before it entered the warehouse. Shortly afterwards, Cocking was detained and charged with robbery. He denied all knowledge of the parcels. [34]

At around mid-day on Sunday 16 September 1861, Harvey Wilde, proprietor of a billiards saloon, paid a visit to his Mulberry Street office, to check if any letters had recently been delivered, that were needing his attention. Arriving at the foot of the stairs that led up from the street, he found that the door had been forced open, and it became clear that there had been an overnight burglary. His office had been ransacked: cupboards lay open, with the contents scattered around. But to his relief, Mr Wilde found that nothing had been stolen – probably, he assumed, because there was really nothing there that a thief would find worth stealing.

But then he noticed that intruders had also broken into the adjoining property, which belonged to Rhodes Brothers, silver plate manufacturers. Mr Wilde was sure that there would be many valuable items in this warehouse, so he informed the police, who sent an urgent message to John and Thomas Rhodes, asking them to attend. Their inspection revealed that fortunately, the burglars' progress through the building had apparently been slowed down by a series of locked internal doors. But even so, a glass display cabinet and an oak chest had been broken open and a large collection of the firm's most valuable products had been removed.

It seemed, however, that the intruders had been intending to return and resume their raid, because apart from the items that had gone missing, many other items had been gathered together in a large basket concealed near the stairs. Detectives Brayshaw and Airey inferred that the burglars, assuming the property would remain closed, had planned to return on the Sunday, to take the basket away. Mr Wilde's chance visit had put an end to their scheme.

So, a search began, which produced information that William Holmes, a man with a previous history of burglary, had been seen in a local beer house, attempting to sell some of the silver-plated items on the list of stolen goods. He was apprehended, and these items were positively identified as having come from the Rhodes Brothers' warehouse. [35]

※　※　※

In front of many old terraced houses, built facing directly onto the street, there would be a rectangular opening in the pavement, protected by a lockable iron grate or a hinged wooden trap door, through which coal and other goods could be delivered directly into the cellar. If the premises were used as a shop, the pavement opening would be larger, to allow through boxes, sacks, and crates – and sometimes burglars.

※　※　※

John Haslam, his sons and their shop assistant, Eliza Hessey, lived on Cemetery Road a short walk away from Mr Haslam's lock-up grocery shop on Ecclesall Road. One evening during February 1862, Eliza secured the shop in the evening, as usual; but next morning, she found that the shop had been robbed. Burglars had entered the shop through the cellar grate and carried away some cheeses and five large hams. So, Eliza hurried to inform the police.

Enquiries made by Detectives Airey and Leonard, that morning, led them to the *Portland Arms* public house in Rockingham Street. As they were walking up the street towards the pub (they learned later), a man sitting in the tap room, at the window overlooking the street, had cried out "There's Airey and Leonard coming!" [36] John Dodd, sitting at the next table, with Joseph Youle and William Newsome, exclaimed "We're done!" And they were.

The landlord's wife, Mrs Emma Sayles, and her servant, Ann Cutler, told the detectives that Dodd, Youle, and Newsome had turned up at the pub earlier that morning, carrying the cheese and the hams, asking if they could put them in the cellar. Because she knew the men, Mrs Sayles had innocently agreed to this. About an hour later, two customers who had come in for a drink had been approached by Youle and taken down into the cellar. When they came back up to the tap room, they were overheard discussing buying some of the stolen goods and negotiating prices.

In court, Mr Haslam and Eliza Hessey identified the cheese and the hams as those stolen from the shop, witnesses testified to the events in the *Portland Arms*, and another witness described how on the previous evening, he had seen the accused men in the pub, planning the robbery. [37]

Grocer John Goddard and his family lived above their shop in Granville Street. At about three o'clock, one morning during June 1861, Mr Goddard's sleep was disturbed by a familiar noise from the shop below: the rattle of his flour scales. He quickly went down to investigate but couldn't get through to the shop because the stairs door had been wedged shut from the other side. While he was trying to force it open, the burglars made their escape. When he finally got through to the shop, Mr Goddard could see that several hams and flitches of bacon, and large quantities of tea and tobacco had been taken. Later, it was found that although the burglars had entered the premises by levering out the cellar grate, they had afterwards replaced it, so as not to attract the attention of any passers-by or patrolling policemen.

When a report of the burglary reached the police station, Detective Officer Airey set off towards Granville Street. His journey took him along Harmer Lane, where he found a trail of salt along the pavement. He followed the trail (shaken from the preserved meat) until it led to a house owned by Henry Bradshaw. Airey found that Bradshaw had gone out, leaving his wife, Sarah, at home alone. Mrs Bradshaw allowed the detective to search the house, where he duly found all the stolen goods.

Bradshaw was later arrested and charged with burglary. But it was clear to the detectives that he could not have made off with so many heavy items on his own. While making wider enquiries, they found a witness who, during the evening before the burglary, had seen Bradshaw in a local pub in deep conversation with a man named George Challenger (alias George Baker). This evidence would be insufficient to secure a conviction in court, without being supported by other information. The required support was eventually achieved through a bizarre coincidence.

While the burglars were still in the shop, after they had gathered their stolen items together and were ready to make their getaway, Challenger had unlocked and opened the front door – to find himself face to face with the patrolling policeman, Constable Thomas Mastin. As he approached the door, the constable had heard the sound of a key turning in the lock. So, he paused, to see what would happen next. As he stood there, a man emerged from the doorway and calmly wished him "Good morning!" PC Mastin, assuming he was in conversation with the shop's proprietor, replied, "Good morning! You've got up in good time, this morning!". The man replied, "Yes!" then went back into the shop, leaving PC Mastin to resume his beat. Bradshaw and Challenger waited inside the shop for a few minutes, before making a very hurried escape.

Challenger's apparent good fortune in being saved by his cool nerves and quick thinking, soon became his undoing. A few days later, following up the witness's report of his rendezvous with Bradshaw in the pub, Challenger was detained by the police. By then, PC Mastin had reported his conversation at the shop door and, to his embarrassment, realised that the unknown man with whom he had exchanged pleasant greetings, had been Bradshaw's accomplice. But this brief encounter had enabled the constable to have a good look at Challenger and hear his voice.So now, at the police station, he was able to identify him as one of the burglars – and the detectives' evidence was complete. [38]

Footnotes

25.   1859: SDN, November 5; SDT, November 7, and December 8; SI, December 10.
26.   1860: SDT, May 1, 4, 17; SI, May 5, 19.
27.   1862, SI, November 18, 29; SDT, November 25, 29, and December 13.
28.   1865: SDT, September 18, 19, 23, and December 15; SI, September 18, 19, 23; Leeds Times, December 16; Leeds Mercury, December 16.
29.   1862: SI, September 1, 6.
30.   1863: SDT, February 13, 20; SI, February 13, 21.
31.   1862: SI, February 11, and March 4.
32.   1863: SDT, October 16, 24; SI, October 22, 24, 31.
33.   1864: SI, October 29, November 5, and December 3; SDT October 31.
34.   1861: SDT, January 17, 19; SI, January 19, and March 2.
35.   1861: SDT, September 17; SI, November 12, 15, 16.
36.   Just as policemen could recognise and name habitual criminals, policemen were equally well-known to the town's criminals. Depending on the occasion, this could, be either an advantage or a handicap.
37.   1862: SDT: February 13, 15, 27; SI, February 27, and March 8.
38.   1861: SDT, June 8, 14, 19, and July 16; SI, June 15, 22; Yorkshire Gazette, August 17.

Norfolk Row

During the nineteenth century, when Dr Wood's stable was burgled,
these buildings were private residences. Now, comprising offices,
hairdressers' salons and coffee shops, etc., the row has survived to
offer an old-fashioned contrast to its modern surroundings.

CHAPTER FOUR

NO HIDING PLACE

The south side of Norfolk Row is now occupied by shops, cafés and
offices; but in Victorian times these buildings were private residences.
Late one Saturday night in November 1861, a thief broke into a stable
behind one of these houses – the property of Dr Hugh Wood, a
well-known Sheffield surgeon. Next morning, Dr Wood's coachman,
William Gouldsbury, discovered the theft: a pair of reins, a horse
cover, and a large bag of mixed oats and barley had been stolen. But
fortunately, he also found a clue. In the darkness, the escaping thief
had failed to notice that the bag was leaking; so, while carrying off his
loot, he had dropped a trail of horse food behind him. The coachman
was now able to follow the trail from Norfolk Row, across to a house in
Lord Street.

Dr Wood reported the burglary and informed the police of the
address where the trail ended. Shortly afterwards, Detective Officer Airey,
accompanied by Constable John Allwood went to Lord Street, to have a
word with the house's surprised owner, William Keyworth. When asked
why he appeared to be in possession of all the stolen items, Keyworth
denied knowing anything about them; but in court, he pleaded guilty.[39]

One Saturday in February 1850, while Detective Ephraim Sills was on duty in Sheffield town centre, he noticed two men behaving suspiciously in West Bar. They were paying visits to all the shops along the street – but for no obvious purpose. After emerging from one shop, they immediately entered the next, and so on. The following Monday, Sills saw these men again, so he shadowed them, as they worked their way along the streets. When they reached Arundel Street, while one of the men waited outside, the other entered the shop. When he came out, they continued walking along the street together, while Detective Sills went into the shop, to ask Mr. Swift what reason this man had given for his visit. He had given his name as George Turner, and said he was a joiner, living at Heeley. He claimed to have fallen on hard times and was now begging for money, so that he could set up his workshop again and resume his trade. To support his claim, Turner had shown Mr Swift a letter, describing his misfortunes and appealing for charitable donations. Beneath, were the signatures of about a dozen alleged supporters and the sums of money they had supposedly already given to this worthy cause.

Detective Sills made enquiries about "George Turner" and found sufficient evidence to believe that this man was an impostor, and that the signatures on the letter were forgeries. So, he traced "George Turner" to his lodging house, where he arrested him. Turner protested his innocence, though he knew that the letter, still in his possession, would prove him guilty. So, while he was being led by the detective towards the police station, Turner made a desperate attempt to rid himself of this key evidence. He pulled it out of his pocket and tore it into pieces, which he scattered on the footpath. The detective promptly foiled this attempt to destroy evidence by carefully collecting all the scattered fragments. When they reached the police station, Sills joined the pieces together again, and the re-formed letter was presented in court, where Turner – now under his real name, Hugh McDonald – was charged with begging for money under false pretences. Despite being positively identified by Mr. Swift, who gave evidence of their conversation in his shop, McDonald most emphatically denied the whole of Detective Sill's statement – but without success.[40]

One night during February 1862, burglars broke into Mr George Ellison's grocer's shop along Powell Street, via his cellar trap door. They stole a large barrel of butter, quantities of soap and candles, and a considerable amount of money. To conceal evidence of their crime, the burglars closed the trap door again, before making their escape. But next morning, when Mr Ellison woke up, he discovered the burglary and reported it to the police. Detectives Airey, Brayshaw and Leonard began making enquiries. Using their knowledge of Sheffield's habitual criminals, they soon apprehended three men – Peter Flinn (who had just been released from prison, having served a 12-month sentence for shop burglary), Thomas Hemmings, and George Hoyes – at their lodgings in Scotland Street. The men's protests of innocence were overshadowed by the discovery of all the stolen items in their possession. [41]

In 1855, staff at Sheffield's Victoria station noticed that some of the parcels brought in to be delivered by train were going missing. Placards were erected around the station advertising a reward of £10 for information that might lead to solving the mystery, but with no success. Charles Hobson, a 13-year-old boy employed in the telegraph office, fell under suspicion because, several times, after a train had pulled into the station, he had been reprimanded for loitering close to its guard's van (where parcels were stored during the journey). The latest parcel to have disappeared contained nine valuable gold and silver watches that Isaac Moss, a watchmaker and jeweller with a shop in the High Street, was sending to Thomas Russell, a watchmaker in Liverpool.

Normally, the railway's routine precautions ensured that parcels remained secure while passing through the station. Each time parcels passed from one stage to the next, their details (in this case, the watches' serial numbers) were checked and recorded. The precautions virtually formed a crime prevention plan and, though on this occasion they failed to prevent Charles Hobson's nimble theft, they proved central to its solution. Much credit was due to the train's guard, George Whittaker, who regularly and conscientiously checked his parcel load. On discovering that Mr Moss's parcel had been removed from the train, Guard Whitaker cleverly used electric telegraphy while *en route* to Liverpool, to report the theft to the authorities back in Sheffield.

When questioned, Charles Hobson attempted to evade detection by feeding fictitious information to his employers, to the police, and to the pawnbroker at the shop where he attempted to pledge one of the watches (not realising that its serial number would be checked). But, calling on his many years' experience of criminals and safe hiding places, Detective Inspector Samuel Linley believed none of Hobson's lies, and didn't need help to predict where the missing watches would eventually be found: in Charles Hobson's bedroom. [42]

One Wednesday in March 1859, at about nine o'clock in the evening, William Rodgers walked along to his local beer house in Broomhall Street. In his waistcoat pocket he carried a gold watch, secured by a heavy gold chain, and he was wearing a diamond ring on his finger.

The owner of the beer house, James Chadburn, and his assistant, Ann, sat with Mr Rodgers, keeping him company as he drank, until he left to go home at about one o'clock. But when he reached home, in consequence of something his wife said, Mr Rodgers found that he had been robbed of both his watch and his ring. Next morning, at about eight o'clock, he returned to the beer house, to confront Chadburn and his assistant. He told them he had been robbed the night before and asked if they knew anything of the articles. They both denied knowledge of them, though Chadburn suggested that Mr Rodgers must have lost the watch and the ring as he walked home down Broomhall Street.

Unhappy with these denials, Mr Rodgers reported his loss to

the police, and in due course Mr Jackson, the Chief Constable[43], accompanied by Detective Officer Brayshaw, visited the beer house, to interview Chadburn about the incident. Chadburn said he knew nothing about it but had no objection to his house being searched. He accompanied Mr Jackson and Officer Brayshaw, as they went ahead with their search. On the top floor, in an attic which appeared to be used as a storeroom, they found a mattress reared against a wall. Mr Jackson asked Chadburn to remove the mattress. In response, he laid it flat on the floor. Brayshaw then carried it across to the other side of the room and while doing so, noticed that one of the floor boards had recently been taken up. This board had been partially covered by the mattress when it leaned against the wall; and when Chadburn had laid the mattress on the floor, he had again contrived to lay it over the board. Officer Brayshaw took up the board and put his hand down into the cavity as far as he could reach. He felt something and lifted it out, revealing Mr Rodgers' watch and ring, wrapped in paper.

Chadburn was taken to the Town Hall, still denying any knowledge of the theft. He claimed that the watch and ring had been given to him three or four days previously by a woman whom he did not know.

In court, positive evidence of Mr Rodgers' ownership of the watch and ring was confirmed. He told the court that when he left the beer house, he "knew what he was about". In other words, he claimed he had remained sober. But while being questioned, he admitted that Ann had sat close to him and at one point had put her arm round him – though he couldn't be sure of what exactly happened. At a further court hearing, Chadburn pleaded guilty to the charge of stealing Mr Rodgers' watch and ring.[44]

At about six o'clock on Sunday evening 14 October 1860, Thomas Dawson set off from his home in Monmouth Street, to go to church. He left his house empty, but both front and back doors were locked. When he returned, about two hours later, the doors had been forced open, and the house had been burgled. Some money had been taken, together with a gold watch and chain, a silver teapot, a set of spoons, and several other articles.

The following day, acting on information received, Detective Officer Robert Airey, accompanied by Sergeant John Allwood, began a search for Joseph Clark, a man they suspected of being involved in this burglary. They found him in bed, in a Duke Street lodging house owned by John Dempsey. In the bedroom, the officers noticed that the floorboards had been recently disturbed. Airey lifted one of the boards, reached underneath with his arm and drew out the stolen spoons and the gold watch.[45] Allwood then found the silver teapot in John Dempsey's bedroom chimney. In custody, when charged with the theft, Clark stated that he had bought these articles the previous evening, from two men at the *Sawmill Tavern* but he did not know their names. [46]

One Saturday afternoon in May 1866, Miss Margaret Weild and her sister, Maria, were waiting on the platform at Manchester's London Road Station[47], ready to catch the three o'clock train to Sheffield. They watched as their luggage – a large, brown japanned tin box filled with clothes – was safely loaded into the luggage van. But then, by mistake, they climbed into the wrong carriage. So, their train left without them. A message was quickly telegraphed through to Sheffield's Victoria station, explaining what had happened, asking for the box to be looked after for an hour or so, until the sisters arrived on the four o'clock train.

But when Margaret and Maria arrived in Sheffield, their box could not be found. It had been stolen from the platform by James Rogers, a local thief with previous convictions for stealing clothes. He took it to the home of Mary Needham, in Norfolk Lane. Mary knew Rogers but was not expecting delivery of a box, so she asked him why he had brought it. He told her that it belonged to an actress who was coming to Sheffield to perform at one of the theatres, and she would be arriving later. Mary was suspicious. She noticed that the box had already been unlocked, but when she mentioned this to Rogers, he made no reply.

Though she waited patiently, no-one, actress or otherwise, came to collect the box. So, the following day, she contacted the police. Detective Officers Brayshaw and Battersby took the box to the police station. They knew Rogers and, after a quick search, found him in Barker's Pool. At the police station, his pockets revealed a handkerchief embroidered "M. T. Weild", a brass lock, and a card addressed, "Miss Weild, passenger, Sheffield". When charged with stealing the box from the Victoria station, Rogers confessed and added that he had pledged one of Miss Weild's dresses at Forster's pawn shop in Pinstone Street, receiving 12 shillings in return.

In court, the three o'clock train's guard, Joseph Holmes, confirmed that he had placed Miss Weild's box on the platform at the Victoria station, and John Henry Law, Mr. Forster's apprentice at the pawn shop, confirmed the Saturday evening transaction. [48]

At about two o'clock, one morning in August 1860, a patrolling officer on duty in the town centre discovered that the door of Joseph Rodgers' cutlery warehouse had been levered open. He at once reported this, and Mr. Rodgers was asked to come and inspect the premises, to check his losses. An intruder had forced open a set of drawers and had stolen a finished and packed collection of spring knife cutlery.

When Detective Officers Brayshaw and Airey began their enquiries, they were led to suspect a man with a record of burglary, John Gillott, a scissor grinder who lived in Silver Street. The officers searched Gillott's house, where they found a collection of burglary tools, including a chisel which precisely matched the marks gouged into Mr Rodgers' drawer. On this evidence, Brayshaw and Airey, in conjunction with Inspector Sills, apprehended Gillott on suspicion of theft. But the detectives could find no sign of the stolen cutlery. After making a second, very thorough search of Gillott's house, they had still found nothing, until Brayshaw found a key that had been carefully concealed in a small hole in the cellar wall.

The detectives had noticed that the house next door was unoccupied. Knowing that thieves often used vacant properties for temporary storage of stolen goods, they now suspected that this key might solve the mystery. Their suspicions were correct: it unlocked the door of the unoccupied house, in which, after a further careful search, they found the whole of the cutlery stolen from Mr. Rodgers' warehouse.[49]

During the autumn of 1861, the firm of Henry Wilkinson and Company, Norfolk Street, suffered some thefts of silver, both in the form of ingots and as manufactured products. Suspicions were expressed by senior members of staff, that Albert Glossop, who had recently been taken on as an apprentice, could be the culprit.

When Detective Officers Airey, Brayshaw and Leonard began their enquiry, Glossop soon admitted that he had been stealing. But the detectives persisted with their questioning because it was obvious to them that their investigation would not be confined to the crime of theft; the stolen silver would now be in the hands of a receiver. Glossop confessed that he had set up a working relationship with another Wilkinson's employee, George Dearman, who had also been stealing silver (though he, so far, had managed to avoid detection). Glossop told the detectives that Dearman had accompanied him on several occasions, to the shop of a local jeweller, Michael Levinson, where they negotiated valuations and deals.

The detectives then focused their attention on Levinson's trading practices, revealing enough evidence to charge the jeweller with receiving silver stolen from Wilkinson's. Specific items recovered from Levinson's shop were positively identified by Mr Joseph Littlewood, Wilkinson's manager, because they bore unique tool marks. The type of silver was also significant: Mr Littlewood believed it would not be found elsewhere within the industry in Sheffield.

The three defendants appeared at the York Assizes where they were found guilty. Before passing sentence, the judge, Mr Justice Wightman,

JOSEPH
RODGERS & SONS
LIMITED.
6 Norfolk Street
SHEFFIELD.
REGISTERED
TRADE
MARK
GRANTED 1682
BEST ELECTRO PLATE
ON NICKEL SILVER
62783.

commented on the social harm committed by thieves and, possibly
the greater harm committed by receivers – because their collaboration
encouraged thieves to continue stealing.[50]

One Friday night in November 1857, William Blackburn's hat shop in
Chapel Walk was burgled: drawers and cupboards were broken open
and a box of clothing was stolen; but the main item carried off by the
burglars was Mr Blackburn's iron safe, containing money and various
items of silver and gold, including a lady's gold ring. Though the safe
had been taken away on a hand cart (stolen from a neighbouring
shop along Chapel Walk) its heavy weight indicated that the burglary
couldn't have been committed by one person alone.

A few days later, the safe was found empty, with its door levered
off, in a brick yard on Wostenholm Road. A hammer and crowbar
lay nearby. Initial enquiries led police to believe that a man named
John Martin had been involved in this crime but, unfortunately, he
had just left Sheffield. As a member of the West Yorkshire Militia,
he had been required to join his regiment in Doncaster. A policeman
was urgently sent to Doncaster, to apprehend Martin and bring him
back to Sheffield. Meanwhile, Detective Robert Airey went to search
Martin's house, where he found Ann Martin, his wife, sporting a gold
ring, which was later identified by Mr Blackburn as one of those stolen
from his shop.

A team comprising Inspector Linley and Detective Officers
Brayshaw and Airey then conducted a search to collect information
with which they reconstructed the events that followed the burglary.
They found that John Martin had a brother, William, who lived in a
house on Landsdowne Road. Early on Saturday morning, less than two
hours after the burglary, John Martin and two other men had arrived
at William's house, bringing the safe with them, on a hand cart. They
had asked William if he would hide the safe in his cellar until they
returned in the evening to collect it. During the day, they had hired

a carrier, William Hall, to bring his donkey and cart to Landsdowne Road in the evening, to carry what they simply described to him as "a heavy load" to a brick yard, on Wostenholm Road. John Martin denied his involvement in this crime – until he appeared in court, where he pleaded guilty to the burglary at Mr Blackburn's shop. But his two accomplices – the two "other men" – remained at large.

Although the Sheffield detective team normally aimed to complete its investigations quickly, leaving no "loose ends", there were occasions when, even after months of hard work, a case could remain unresolved. When this happened, full details would be put in a "pending" file so that, at some point in the future, enquiries could be quickly resumed.

The Chapel Walk robbery became one of these cases. The two men suspected of involvement had left town immediately after helping to move Mr Blackburn's safe to the brick yard. Six months later, hoping the coast was now clear, they returned to Sheffield, attempting to remain unnoticed. But William Glossop was found and detained in West Street by Police Constable John Salvin, and George ("Fancy") Brown was spotted and apprehended by Detective Officer Richard Brayshaw at a public house in the Hartshead area.

In court, both Brown and Glossop admitted having been John Martin's accomplices – so, the case could finally be closed.[51]

In 1863, the South Yorkshire Railway began building an extension to link its tracks to the Manchester, Sheffield and Lincolnshire Railway. The work was being carried out by Benjamin Verity, a Mexborough contractor, who had established a site office at Darnall. On Friday night, 9 January, these premises were broken into, and about 60kg of blasting powder were stolen. The police conducted a search of the area which led to the discovery by Constable William Toulson of a barrel and three bags of blasting powder. The "safe place" chosen by the thief was a hamper, hidden under a manure heap in a field near Handsworth. PC Toulson also discovered a trail of footprints left by three men and a donkey. He covered some of the footprints, protecting them so that they would remain undamaged and available as evidence, if required.[52]

The police sought help from George Brewett, an employee of the firm that had supplied the blasting powder to the contractors. They took Mr Brewett during daytime to the field where the cache had been discovered. He confirmed the powder's identity, and then they carefully returned it to its hiding place. Next, Detective Officers Richard Brayshaw and James Winn established an overnight watch in the field, suspecting that the thief would soon return to move the blasting powder to somewhere more convenient for whatever purpose he planned to use it. This duly happened. In the darkness, a cutlery worker, George Drabble, entered the field, retrieved the bags and the barrel from their hiding place – and was promptly apprehended.[53]

※ ※ ※

As well as feeding helpful information to the police, members of the public could sometimes take an active part in assisting officers in the execution of their duty.

※ ※ ※

On Wednesday evening, 26 October 1859, Willoughby Howe, landlord of *The Cock Inn* in Oughtibridge, was walking up the Victoria Station's approach road, on his way to catch a train home,[54] when he met a man and woman coming down the road towards him. As they drew closer, Mr Howe stepped to one side, to allow the couple to pass him. But they then subjected him to a garotte robbery – a particularly nasty attack on the throat, not fatal but vicious enough to leave the victim choked and helpless. While the man seized Mr Howe from behind and threw an arm tightly around his throat, the woman emptied his pockets of all his money, and ripped away the large woollen rug that he was carrying. The rug was new – Mr Howe had purchased it only the day before, from Benjamin Richards' draper's shop in the Market Place – and it was made of a distinctive material with a fancy pattern.

The couple then ran off, leaving Mr Howe weakened and distressed. But fortunately, John Hempsall, a Sheffield butcher, who had been following Mr Howe up the road, had witnessed the incident and, as they ran past him, had taken a close look at the attackers and noted their appearance.

Two or three days later, after making enquiries, Detective Officers Airey and Brayshaw paid a call on John Lee at his house in Hawley Croft. They found him in his bed, across which was laid a suit, newly made from cloth with a fancy pattern. Lee claimed that he had bought the suit a week ago, but he couldn't remember where. However, the detectives' enquiries revealed that Lee's suit had been made by a local tailor, Joseph Sykes, who told them how Lee had presented him with a rug and asked him to convert it into a suit. The cloth's distinctive pattern enabled Benjamin Richards to identify it as having been made from the rug he sold to Mr Howe.

At the police station, Airey and Brayshaw arranged an identity parade, at which Mr Hempsall picked out Lee as the man he had seen running away from the railway station.[55]

On 4 November 1861, Thomas Owen, a Sheffield butcher, went to Rotherham cattle market, where he bought six beef cows. The animals were already branded with the previous owner's initials "JND" to which Owen now added his own identifying mark: a red cross. His friend, Charles Corbett, drove the cattle from the market to Owen's pasture at Ecclesfield. Two days later, Owen sent one of his employees, John Parkin, to collect the cattle and bring them closer into Sheffield. But when he reached the pasture, Parkin discovered that one of the cows was missing: he returned to Sheffield with only five.

Mr Owen immediately reported this theft to the police. Shortly afterwards, Detective Officers Robert Airey and Richard Brayshaw travelled out to Ecclesfield, to start making enquiries. They discovered that an Ecclesfield butcher, Thomas Muff, had slaughtered a beast on the previous day. So, they thought it would be worth having a word with him – particularly when some local people assured them that Muff normally purchased carcasses; he did not slaughter his animals. With their suspicions increasing, the detectives interviewed Muff, who agreed that he had recently slaughtered a beast, but denied having been involved in its theft. He told them that he had bought the cow from a farmer who lived in Kimberworth Park – though he did not know the farmer's name.

Realising that it would be difficult to identify an animal from its slaughtered carcass, the detectives returned to Sheffield; but they made another journey to Ecclesfield, the next day – this time, taking Mr Owen with them – to concentrate their efforts on finding the animal's hide. They again interviewed Muff. He told them he had given the hide to his business partner, William Sagar, a butcher who lived in Chapeltown. So, the detectives and Mr Owen made their way across to Chapeltown, where they interviewed Mr Sagar. He denied having a partnership with Muff, and firmly stated that he had not received a hide from him. They therefore returned to Ecclesfield, where Muff eventually confessed that he had been deliberately misleading them. In fact, the hide was in a sack, still bearing the marks "JND" and a red cross, in Muff's back kitchen. [56]

Footnotes

39. 1861: SDT, November 5; SI, November 5, 9.
40. 1850: SI, February 9.
41. 1862: SI, February 14, 15, and March 8; SDT, February 19, and March 5.
42. 1855: SI, February 24, and March 3.
43. The Chief Constable regularly involved himself in practical police work, by going out with his officers to crime scenes, and by attending court hearings.

44. 1859: April 22, and May 21; SI, April 23, and May 21; SDN, May 21.
45. The use of cavities under floorboards for hiding stolen goods, though popular with thieves and familiar to detectives, seems to have remained largely unknown to law-abiding readers. So, in *The Second Stain*, published in October 1904, over forty years after the thefts from William Rodgers and Thomas Dawson, Sherlock Holmes was able to impress Dr Watson by tracing a stolen letter to where it had been deposited by Eduardo Lucas, under floorboards in his Westminster home.
46. 1860: SI, October 20, 27, and December 8; SDT, October 26, and December 5.
47. Now *Manchester Piccadilly Station*.
48. 1866: SDT, May 25, 26, 29, and June 2; SI, May 25, and June 2.
49. 1860: SDT, August 28, and October22; SI, August 25, September 1, and October 27.
50. 1861: SI, November 9, 12, 16, and December 13, 14; SDT, December 13; York Gazette, December 14.
51. 1857: SDT, November 12, 16, 28; SI, November 14, 21.
    AND
    1858: SDT, May 5, 6; SI, May 8, 22.
52. Before the 1890s, although detectives would have noted the dirty and greasy smudges found at crime scenes or on recovered stolen goods, they would have been unable to use them as aids to identification. Scotland Yard set up a Fingerprint Department in 1895 but its early work was confined to comparing fingerprints, rather than using them for absolute identification: a report (based on naked-eye comparison) might say that, for example, the prints found on object *X* were made by the same person who left prints on object *Y*. Their reliability as evidence in court was resisted until objective, scientific analysis was introduced. Meantime, if they wished to prove a person's attendance at a crime scene, detectives were limited to comparing a suspect's footwear with the fresh footprints found at the scene – and then only if it lay within soft ground or lying snow.
53. 1863: SI, January 14, 16, and March 5, 7; SDT, January 17, and March 5.
54. Mr Howe would have been planning to catch a local train service from the Victoria Station, via Wadsley Bridge, to Oughtibridge – a 9-minute journey.
55. 1859: SDN, November 5, and December 9; SDT, November 7; SI, December 10; Leeds Intelligencer, December 10.
56. 1861: SI, November 11, 16, and December 17, 21; SDT, November 11, 12, 14, and December 17.

St James's Row

When tailor James Storey and his family were residents here,
their neighbours included (in the building with the large end gable)
Sheffield's Charity School for Poor Girls, built by public subscription in 1786.

CHAPTER FIVE

JOINING FORCES

During the 1840s and 1850s, there was great public interest in *electric telegraphy*, a recent invention that offered high-speed, long-distance transmission of written messages. Manufacturers, traders, news organisations and railway companies were among the first commercial users, followed by the the country's police forces, who began to use it for quick communication with colleagues outside their own local areas.[57]

Faced with the task of establishing a network of wires, the telegraph companies struck a fortunate deal with the railway companies. Wherever the terrain had allowed, railway companies had built their tracks straight and direct, to shorten journey times. By coincidence, the telegraph companies also wanted to keep their wires short, to prevent too much weakening of the electrical signals. So, wherever possible, telegraphic wires ran alongside railway lines – a combination that formed a sight familiar to train passengers for over a hundred years.

The installation of telegraph poles and wires progressed steadily, radiating from the London hub. But at that time, Sheffield's hilly landscape was preventing the town from having a direct railway route to London; and this same problem now delayed Sheffield's connection to the telegraphy network. [58]

Local newspapers kept readers informed of progress [59, 60] until, during the autumn of 1846, Sheffield finally achieved its connection to the nationwide electric telegraphy system and the Police Force joined the town's other organisations in enjoying its benefits.

⌘ ⌘ ⌘

In Sheffield, as in many towns across the country, hundreds of young women worked "in service" as domestic staff, performing household duties for well-off families. Many were content with their roles, but others disliked performing menial tasks, and rebelled against rules they considered too harsh. Mary Ann Slaughter was employed as a maid in the home of Sheffield tools manufacturer John Buxton and his family; but she didn't like being ordered around. Instead, she wanted to go to London, to join her sister and enjoy a better life.

An unexpected opportunity occurred one day, when Mr Buxton's wife hurried out to the shops, leaving her bunch of house keys behind on the kitchen table. Mary Ann, sensing that here was an advantage that shouldn't be wasted, slipped the keys into her pocket. By chance, she discovered that one of them opened a cupboard in her attic bedroom, inside which she found a purse containing £9 – more than enough to pay her train fare to London! She didn't hesitate.

Next morning, the Buxton family woke up to find that their maid was missing. But they knew that she had a sister in London and, guessing that this is where she would be heading, they informed the police. A young woman answering Mary Ann's description had been seen early that morning at the railway station, boarding a London train. So, the Sheffield police quickly arranged for a telegraphic message describing Miss Slaughter's appearance, to be sent to neighbouring towns, particularly those along the train route to London. The message reached Leicester railway station at about a quarter to three in the afternoon, alerting staff to the possibility that a Miss Slaughter would be on board the train due to reach Leicester at three o'clock.

Sergeant John Neale of the Leicester police waited on the station platform as the train from Sheffield drew in. To avoid warning Mary Ann about the surprise lying in store for her, and to stop her making a bid for freedom, he had disguised himself by wearing a porter's great coat over his policeman's uniform. He boarded the train and, from the telegraphed description, soon found Mary Ann. Addressing her by name, he asked why she had come to Leicester. Understandably, she was shocked and became confused – particularly when Sergeant Neale removed the porter's coat, to reveal his true authority. With her plan foiled, Mary Ann realised that her position was hopeless. Sergeant Neale's next task was to escort Miss Slaughter on a return journey to Sheffield. Her feelings were completely understandable: what could be faster than an express train? [61]

Robert and Elizabeth Armstrong lived in Leeds, where they owned a stall in the Kirkgate Market, selling flour and grain. One evening in February 1859, when the market closed, they set off to walk home, carrying the day's takings with them. Along St Peter's Street, as they were about to pass a barber's shop, Mr Armstrong decided to call in for a shave, leaving his wife to continue alone on the short journey back to their house in St Peter's Square. The streets were busy, but Mrs Armstrong assured her husband that she would be safe. Just before she had reached her front door, however, she became yet another victim of a "garotte robbery", when she was attacked by a gang of four young men. Mrs Armstrong, half-strangled and incapable of defending herself, passed out and was left lying on the pavement. When consciousness returned, Mrs Armstrong realised that all her money, amounting to £84, had gone. The Leeds police were called in to investigate but had no success in tracing the men. So, believing (correctly) that the gang might attempt to escape justice by leaving town, they telegraphed a description of the wanted suspects to neighbouring forces.

When this information reached Sheffield, Detective officers Airey and Brayshaw took note of the details and set out on a night-time search of some of the town centre's notorious public houses. In *The Waggon*, they found a group of four men who not only fitted the descriptions telegraphed from Leeds but also stood out from their fellow drinkers: kitted out in brand new suits of fashionable clothes, they were ordering drinks freely and lavishly, as if payment would not be a problem.

Airey and Brayshaw took the men into custody. Details of their arrest were telegraphed to the Leeds police. All the men offered fictitious names, but when the Leeds police studied the information from Sheffield, it was clear that these were the wanted men. In court, it was reported that the Leeds Police Force were grateful to the Sheffield detectives for arresting these men, and were sending Detective Officer Byrne to Sheffield, to take charge of the prisoners. The Sheffield magistrates ordered that the four men should be given up to the Leeds detective when he arrived, to be dealt with through the Leeds court system. [62]

James Storey, a master tailor and woollen draper, lived with his wife and family in a large house and shop on St James's Row. [63] One night in February 1859, Mr Storey retired to bed shortly after midnight, little suspecting the shock he would receive, next morning. Overnight, the house was burgled: rolls of cloth worth about £100 were stolen. The burglar had entered at the back, through the kitchen door. He had silently found his way past the family's bedrooms, through to the front shop and cutting room – and back again – without waking anyone. He had also then stolen a wheelbarrow from one of Mr Storey's neighbours, to help carry away the stolen cloth.

As soon as he discovered his loss, Mr Storey informed the police, and Detective Officer Richard Brayshaw arrived to start searching the premises. He began by inspecting the rear of the house, finding that the burglar had drilled a hole through the kitchen door and then used a saw to cut a circular hole, large enough for an arm to be passed through, to release the locks and bolts on the inside. Brayshaw then found the discarded piece of wood cut from the door and, realising its future value, kept it to be stored as evidence at the police station.

A few days later, acting on received information, Detective officers Airey and Brayshaw, with Detective Officer Winn, went to the *Gipsey King* beerhouse, in Holly Street, kept by John Richardson. His wife and five children were at home, but Richardson himself was out: the detectives were informed that he was watching a prize fight in the Rivelin area.

A search of the premises revealed several rolls of cloth hidden in drawers in various parts of the house, and in the outbuildings. The detectives also discovered a set of housebreaking tools including a jemmy, some skeleton keys, and a drill bit which exactly matched the marks on the piece of wood cut from Mr Storey's back door. Meanwhile, Richardson's friends had somehow informed him of the detectives' visit, so he didn't return home; he fled from Sheffield, far enough away (he hoped) to where the police wouldn't find him.

On 19 February, the *Independent* gave its readers an update:

The active exertions of the police have led to the discovery of a large part of the booty, along with a number of burglarious implements. The person in whose premises the property was discovered is at present out of reach, but it is hoped that he will not long evade the vigilance of the police.

This proved to be the case: the Sheffield police telegraphed information about this crime to their colleagues in the surrounding areas and, about a week later, Richardson was found by the police in Derby. Calling himself John Golding, he had been working at the town's Cotton Lane Ironworks. He was arrested by Inspector Benjamin Firth of the Derbyshire police and taken into custody, where he admitted his real name, confessed that he "had been a fool", and was then escorted back to Sheffield, to face trial.

In court, Mr. Storey identified several of the pieces of stolen cloth by both their appearance, and the way they were cut. Richardson's defence consisted of an account of how, two months ago, two men had come to his house, asking for a loan of 10 shillings, with some rolls of cloth as a surety. Later, having spent this money, the men returned with more cloth, asking for a further loan. On both occasions, Richardson said, he had accepted the cloth and stored it where the police found it. He claimed that he knew nothing about the burglary tools; and William Fretson, his attorney, tried to throw doubt on Mr Storey's identification of the cloth and suggested that the police might have planted the drill bit in Richardson's house. The jury were not persuaded. [64]

In 1859, two Sheffield boys, John Barker and John Pickering, travelled to Liverpool, in search of adventure. In the Waterloo Dock, they came across a Greek ship, the brig *Calliope*. They went aboard and asked the captain if they could work their passage on the ship when it made its return voyage to Greece. They were duly taken on as cabin boys. Free to explore the ship before it set sail, the boys found their way into the captain's apartments, where they discovered his sea chest. Opening it, they found among other items, a bag containing a hundred gold sovereigns. They stole the bag, then (in the words of the *Sheffield Daily Telegraph*) "the temptation being too much for them, they divided the spoil, and the same night left the ship and returned to Sheffield".

The ship's captain reported the theft to the Liverpool police, who telegraphed an urgent message to Sheffield's Chief Constable, and a search began. Back in Yorkshire, the boys kept a low profile, while at the same time spending their money (though not all of it: about £50 was recovered) but both were apprehended and – again, according to the *Telegraph*, – "The chase caused no little excitement, and the successful issue reflects credit upon both the Liverpool and Sheffield detectives." [65]

In 1862, another theft brought these two police forces together again in solving a crime; but on this occasion, the initiative arose in Sheffield, and interest was focused on the receiver rather than the thief.

In December, Mrs Mary Heap enjoyed attending a local charity concert at Hope Hall [66] in Liverpool; but on returning home, she discovered that she no longer had her gold watch. The loss was reported to the Liverpool police, who telegraphed a description of the watch to other northern police forces. Three weeks later, while searching the Sheffield home of Matthew Green (a known receiver), Detectives Airey and Brayshaw came across a gold watch. In the circumstances, they realised that this was not Green's property; so, back at the police station, they checked the watch against their lists of stolen items. It appeared to match the description of Mrs Heap's watch, recently telegraphed from Liverpool. In due course, Mrs Heap positively identified the watch, so Green was taken to Liverpool, to face trial on a charge of receiving the watch, knowing it to have been stolen. [67]

Joseph Gratton, a Bakewell watchmaker and jeweller, lived above his shop on Bridge Street. During the early hours of 10 April 1863, Mr Gratton was roused from his sleep by a loud crashing sound. He went downstairs to find that his shop front had been attacked and emptied of items of silverware and jewellery and a large number of gold rings. He heard the footsteps of someone running away but didn't see who it was. Superintendent Rust and Detective Officer Hilton of the Derbyshire police investigated this case; but despite travelling many miles in search of the thief, they had no success. However, details of this crime were recorded and circulated to neighbouring police forces.

Some weeks later, in Sheffield, Detective Richard Brayshaw's attention was caught by an expensive ring being worn by Jane Taylor – a young lady known to be an associate of criminals. The ring's value was far above Jane Taylor's means, so she was questioned, on suspicion of receiving stolen goods. After examining the records of local unsolved robberies, which included descriptions of stolen items, Brayshaw suspected a link between Jane Taylor's ring and the Bakewell robbery. The Sheffield detective team considered this line of enquiry to be worth pursuing and contacted the Derbyshire police, who arranged for Mr Gratton to travel to Sheffield, where he confirmed that the ring was indeed one of those stolen from his shop. Grateful for the Sheffield police force's assistance, their Derbyshire colleagues then took over and shortly afterwards, Jane Taylor appeared at the crown court in Derby.

But the prosecution's charge of receiving was withdrawn, and the trial was halted, when other facts came to light. Jane Taylor was reluctant to divulge how she had acquired the ring because she could not do so without revealing that it had been given to her by James Walter Bearder (*alias* James Edwards, *alias* William Smith). She admitted recognising the ring as stolen property, but her attempt to hand it back to Bearder was prevented when he threatened her with a knife. The prosecutor inferred that the ring had not been given to her as a sign of affection but rather, for Bearder's own purposes, as an act of disposal: he had chosen Taylor as a victim – to be a "safe place".

Bearder was arrested and tried in Derby, not only on Jane Taylor's evidence, but also on his identification by both the landlord of a pub on the route from Sheffield to Bakewell, and the turnpike gatekeeper along the same route, during the evening before the burglary. [68, 69]

In Birmingham on 30 March 1866, a man was robbed of £102 in gold and £65 in Bank of England notes by a couple – a man and a woman – who, it was thought, had then left town in search of somewhere safe. Birmingham's Chief Constable telegraphed a description of the wanted couple (naming them as George and Martha Roberts) to police forces in towns around the country. Sheffield's Chief Constable placed the organisation of a local search in the hands of Detectives Richard Brayshaw and Charles Battersby.[70] Their enquiries led to the discovery of two people matching the given descriptions, who had taken up lodgings in Silver Street.

The detectives kept a close but discreet watch on the lodging house until, after a few days, the pair gave signs that they planned to leave Sheffield. A police presence was then set at the railway station, where the suspects were detained as they entered the station gates. The following day, claiming to be Teddy and Lizzy Clarke, the couple appeared in court before the Sheffield magistrates, who ordered them to be escorted back to Birmingham, where they were put on trial. [71]

An exceptional crime, both in its duration and in the huge value of the stolen material, was committed over many years by two dishonest employees whose work involved handling silver: one in Sheffield and one in Birmingham.

Thomas Smith Evans, previously employed at the firm of Messrs Elkington, Mason & Co., silver platers, Newhall Street, Birmingham, was now employed in Sheffield by Messrs Thomas and Joseph Bradbury, silver platers, of Arundel Street. In this new job, Evans had control over all the silver used by the company. Abusing his trusted position, he regularly deceived his employers, by stealing quantities of silver. Then, rather than risk having his repeated thefts detected in Sheffield, he posted the stolen silver in packets addressed to his collaborator and former colleague, Thomas Dryhurst, who still worked for Elkington and Mason. Dryhurst then sold these batches of silver to Messrs Betts & Co., silver refiners, in St Paul's Square, Birmingham.

Evans and Dryhurst each pocketed half of the money received from Messrs Betts. This arrangement continued for more than ten years, until an employee at Betts, suspecting (although, incorrectly) that Dryhurst was stealing the silver from Elkington and Mason, reported his suspicions to the Birmingham police. Detective Officer John Spokes investigated the situation. When questioned about this allegation, Dryhurst replied that he had stolen nothing from his employers – which was true, because Evans was the thief, in Sheffield, while he, Dryhurst, was receiving silver stolen by his accomplice at Bradbury's.

But Officer Spokes still had strong doubts about Dryhurst's innocence, and he shared his suspicions with Sheffield's Chief Constable. Detective Inspector Airey was given the task of making enquiries locally and collaborating with his colleague in Birmingham. Together, they collected evidence that, despite denials by both the accused men, eventually took them to a trial at the York Assizes. [72]

Footnotes

57. 1848, SI, July 15:

Arrangements are in progress by which a line of the electric telegraph, separate and distinct for police purposes, will be established between the central station of the metropolitan police and the force's suburban stations. This will allow the present expensive and troublesome communication by means of foot and horse messengers, to be avoided. Orders, reports of theft, and other matters, can then be transmitted in a few seconds, and the consequent actions they require can be taken just as promptly. Once the system established in London, its extension to the great towns of the provinces will almost immediately follow.

58. The range of hills south of Sheffield stood in the way of a direct railway route to London. Passengers from Sheffield had first to travel east along the lower Don Valley to Masborough, near Rotherham, where they had to change, to board a train running south along the tracks primarily laid to connect other West Riding towns to London. In 1870, the Bradway tunnel opened, allowing travel due south from Sheffield, along the much shorter route through Dronfield, Chesterfield, and the other towns along today's familiar journey to London.

59. 1846, SI, April 18:

Great progress is made in the continuation of the electric telegraph northward. We mentioned last week that it was in operation between Derby and Masborough. The posts to support the wires are erected as far as Leeds. About as far as the Barnsley Station, the wires are fixed, and up to Wakefield they are in progress.
There is but one thing about the electric telegraph that we have seen with regret, and

that is, that there are no preparations yet visible for its extensions from Masborough to Sheffield. Surely this town is not to be excluded from the advantages of this wonderful and incalculably useful invention?

60. 1846, SI, August 8:

We are glad to see that the Midland Company are erecting posts and putting up the wires for the electric telegraph from Masborough, along the Sheffield and Rotherham line, to Sheffield. This will not only be a great convenience to the servants of the company, but to the public also.

61. 1853: SI, July 9 and August 27; Leicester Chronicle, July 9.

62. 1859: SDN, February 3; SDT, February 4; Leeds Times, February 5, 12; Leeds Intelligencer, February 5.

63. This row of buildings can still be seen today, along the western border of Sheffield Cathedral's graveyard.

64. 1859: SDN, 9 and April 18 and July 19; SI, February 19 and April 23; SDT, February 9.

65. 1859: SDT, November 19; Morning Chronicle, November 21; Western Daily Press, November 21.

66. In 1862, Hope Hall was a concert hall. Today, rebuilt on the same site, stands Liverpool's famous *Everyman Theatre*.

67. 1862, SDT, January 4; SI, January 4, 8, 16; Liverpool Daily Post, January 7; Leeds Mercury, January 16.

68. 1863: SI, May 1, and September 22, 26; Derbyshire Advertiser, September 25 and December 11; Derby Mercury, July 8 and December 16; Derbyshire Courier, December 12; Derbyshire Times, May 2 and July 4 and December 19.

69. James Walter Bearder died in Sheffield, thirty years later. On 1 January 1894, the *Sheffield Daily Telegraph* published a news report under the bizarre headline *Death of a Well-known Criminal*.

It began: "There died in Sheffield on Friday a man who for the last 38 years has devoted his life to breaking the laws of his country and paying the penalty for so doing, and who has succeeded in making for himself a name in the annals of crime." This was followed by a lengthy and detailed *curriculum vitae*, which failed to mention the misery Bearder had inflicted on his countless victims.

70. This case offers an example of how the detective team built up its strength. In 1865, when a vacancy occurred, Sergeant Charles Battersby, after nearly ten years' valuable and reliable service, was promoted to the rank of detective officer. Here, during his first year since promotion, he was paired – as a pupil with his master –

alongside one of the force's most experienced detectives. The years ahead were to bring Charles Battersby further career advancements: in 1876, he was appointed Superintendent of the force's detective division – a post he held this post with distinction until his retirement in 1895.

71. 1866: SDT, April 18, 19, 21; SI, April 18, 19, 21; Birmingham Daily Gazette, April 20.

72. 1866: SI, October 30 and December 17; SDT, November 7 and December 19; Birmingham Daily Gazette, October 30; Birmingham Daily Post, December 18; Leeds Intelligencer, November 7.

The Cutlers' Hall, Church Street

This historic hall, rebuilt in 1832, was often hired by Sheffield's Literary and Philosophical Society for its events – including the meeting in January 1862, when visiting pickpockets met their match.

CHAPTER SIX

VIOLENCE, EVASION AND DENIAL

Regrettably – as still happens today – all police officers in nineteenth-century Sheffield experienced personal assaults. Practically every day, they were required to break up fights in the town's streets and pubs. Offenders would usually be taken to the police station for a night in the cells, followed by a morning in the magistrates' court. Drunken fighters gradually lost their aggression, as exertion and alcohol took their toll; but not until they had tested the officers' physical strength and their psychological skills. They rarely agreed to "go quietly".

⊗ ⊗ ⊗

Working as a team, Detectives Airey and Brayshaw gained a reputation for being able to cope with violence. For this reason, they were chosen in July 1858, to deliver a summons to the home of John Calligan, after he had failed to attend court, to answer a charge of assault. On arriving at the house and stating their business, the officers were greeted with hostile resistance – a ploy to delay their entry to allow Calligan time to escape via the back door. The other occupants of the house then attacked the officers with weapons, inflicting wounds and causing loss of blood. Despite this, the officers arrested two of their assailants and took them to the police station. [73]

But Airey and Brayshaw faced probably their toughest test after a town centre fight, when they had to overcome the resistance displayed by a famous visitor to Sheffield: William "Bendigo" Thompson, a former English champion prize fighter. [74]

In October 1861, now aged 50 and in retirement, Thompson came to spend a few days in Sheffield. But his plans to enjoy a quiet time came to a premature end when he attacked one of his fellow drinkers, Robert Chadwick, in a Castle Street beer house. Upset by this experience, Mr Chadwick made a formal complaint to the police, who were then obliged to arrest Bendigo. They charged him with assault and detained him in the police station pending an appearance before the magistrates, planned for the following day. Unfortunately, Thompson could not keep this appointment because he was still too drunk to answer the charge. So, the hearing was rearranged for the next day. By then, however, the news had spread far and wide, so the courtroom was packed with onlookers, keen to get a glimpse of this celebrity. Some newspaper reporters were said to have travelled from London, especially to cover the case.

When the charge was read, Thompson apologised for his aggression and asked Mr Chadwick to pardon him – which he duly did, and he refrained from pressing his case. Thompson received a reprimand and a fine from the magistrates, so he left the court as a free man and, with the excitement over, the event ended with an anti-climax. Newspapers reported that within about two minutes, the court was deserted. [75]

※ ※ ※

Officers on the beat at night ran a high risk of discovering men in the act of committing a crime. Desperate to escape a prison sentence, especially if they had suffered this experience before, arrested criminals could present much more danger to the police than could brawling pub fighters who simply faced a night in a cell.

One February morning in 1865, Police Constable Thomas Kirk was patrolling along West Bar when, a little after two o'clock, he reached the premises of Thomas Trickett, a licensed victualler. Mr Trickett's front door was secure, so PC Kirk then walked round to the rear. An hour ago, he had checked the door to the back yard, finding it safe. Now, however, when he tried the door, it gave way a little, though it resisted being fully opened. PC Kirk shone his lantern into the keyhole and observed that there was now a key in the lock. Before he could try the door again, a man rushed out from the yard and struck him a savage blow to the head with an iron bar. The constable was stunned and fell to the ground. But before passing out, he caught a look at the man and recognised him. After regaining consciousness, PC Kirk blew his whistle to summon help from a neighbouring beat. The incident was immediately reported to the police station at the Town Hall, and PC Kirk was taken home, where he was later attended by Mr. George Kemp, the Sheffield Police Force's surgeon.

The assault had been carried out by one of Sheffield's habitual offenders: Joseph Young, who, although only 25, had a record of violent crime, going back almost ten years. A few hours later, he was apprehended by Detectives Brayshaw and Whiteley, and taken into custody.

Constable Kirk was in no fit state to attend the court until the following week: Mr Kemp reported that the blow had penetrated the skull and his patient was suffering the effects of excessive bleeding. When Young eventually appeared in court, he protested that he had been at home in his lodgings at the time of the assault; but his witness proved unreliable (unable to read a clock face) so PC Kirk's identification evidence was accepted, rather than this attempted alibi. [76]

※ ※ ※

Violence on a much larger scale occurred occasionally, when terrorist gangs attacked family homes at night, to frighten the occupants and commit robbery. These attacks became known as "outrages".

※ ※ ※

In 1859, an outrage was committed at *Park View*, the home of James
Robinson, a Sheffield brick manufacturer. Mr Robinson's relationships
with his work force had become strained in recent years: employees
regarded his business methods as harsh. So, this crime was thought to
have been driven by a sense of injustice rather than being just a simple
raid in search of valuables.

At about three o'clock on the morning of 20 October, Mr.
Robinson and his wife were woken by a loud noise from the
unoccupied bedroom next door to their own room which, like theirs,
overlooked the front garden. Mr. Robinson ran into the room, finding
it filled with smoke and a strong smell of gunpowder. On the floor lay
a stone ginger beer bottle with a burning fuse in its cork. Fearing an
explosion and, warning his wife not to follow him into the room, Mr.
Robinson extinguished the burning fuse by stamping on it. He then
quickly shepherded his wife and children downstairs, before running
across to the houses nearby, to rouse the occupants and send one of his
workmen off in search of a policeman.

Detective Inspector Sills, who lived in the neighbourhood,
was informed of the outrage, and he, together with with Detective
Officers Brayshaw and Airey went to the Robinsons' house to begin
an investigation. They found that the noise had been caused when the
stone bottle, after smashing through the window, had collided with the
bedroom wall, scattering a mixture of gunpowder, hob-nails, and glass
shards. Its lighted fuse had ignited some of the scattered gunpowder
making a large black mark on the wall but there had been no damage
to the furniture because fortunately, most of the gunpowder had failed
to explode.

Among the scattered debris in the front garden, the detectives
found the remains of two other loaded bottles that had been aimed
at the house windows but had missed their targets and also failed

to explode. James Robinson was no stranger to outrages: he and his property had been attacked twice before and thousands of his bricks had been sabotaged before their manufacture could be completed. But on this occasion, Mr Robinson and his family had a fortunate escape. [77]

In January 1858, an outrage was committed at *Flash House Farm*, at Cawthorne, near Barnsley, the home of widowed 86-year-old Joseph Clarkson, his widowed daughter-in-law, and her children. Seven men wearing smocks and masks, and armed with sticks and bludgeons, broke into the house after midnight. They rushed into Mr Clarkson's bedroom and attacked him savagely; then they entered his daughter-in-law's room and threatened her with violence. The noise made by the burglars as they ransacked the house aroused the family's servant, Richard Marshall, who slept in the attic. He had a gun in his bedroom but no ammunition. Instead, he loaded the gun with an explosive "cap" and took it downstairs to confront the intruders. He pointed the gun at one of the men and fired the cap, making such a frightening explosion that the man fled the scene, taking his companions with him. Richard Marshall was then able to run to the neighbouring properties to raise the alarm and fetch assistance.

The thieves got clear away with their booty, but the police afterwards succeeded in apprehending four of them, leaving three notorious characters at large: George Hebden, Edward Wild and Thomas Jackson.

Sheffield police advertised descriptions of the three wanted men in the national *Police Gazette*, in addition to local network enquiries. Information gathered from these sources led Inspector Ephraim Sills to believe that Wild and Jackson were lying low in Sheffield, in a lodging house in Spring Street. He also had reason to think that the two men were waiting there for Hebden to join them, with the intention of leaving town together, under cover of darkness. A reliable source informed the inspector of a date and time; so, he took up a concealed position close to the house where the two men were lodging, and waited in ambush, hoping to catch all three together.

The alleged departure time – four o'clock in the morning – came and went with no signs of activity. More time passed, and still Hebden had not shown up; so, Sills adjusted his plan: he decided to seize the two men who were still within reach. He approached the door and gave it a gentle tap. Those inside evidently assumed this was the knock of their expected comrade, for it was answered with "All right, come in!" and the door was instantly opened. Sills rushed in and found Wild and Jackson, ready dressed, as if for a journey. He arrested the two men and took them into custody. Hebden was found and arrested shortly afterwards.

Police investigations took an unexpected turn when one of the gang, Joseph Hilton, chose to inform on the others: he told the detectives that he had been persuaded to join the gang against his better judgement. When the raid started, he was so surprised and dismayed by the violence, that he felt compelled to confess his involvement. He revealed to the police how the raid had been planned and executed, and where the gang had afterwards hidden their smocks, masks, and weapons. At the York Assizes, although Hilton's confession was strongly challenged by the attorney representing the other gang members, it strengthened the detectives' evidence and the men were given custodial sentences.

A month after the trial, the imprisoned gang members plotted an escape attempt. Led by Edward Wild, they secretly collected materials from the prisoners' dayroom and used them to construct a rope, intending to use it to climb over the prison walls. Unknown to them, the prison officers had noticed the materials' disappearance from the dayroom and were keeping an eye on the gang members. So, their escape attempt ended very shortly after it began. [78]

In the early hours of Tuesday 9 December 1856, an outrage was committed by a gang of apparently merciless men at *Manor Oaks*, the home of a Sheffield brewer, William Bradley, and his wife, Charlotte. This was on a larger scale and more complicated than those at *Park View* and *Flash House Farm*.

Manor Oaks was well protected: all doors were locked, the windows were defended by shutters lined with iron, and the house was guarded by a dog which, according to the *Sheffield Daily Telegraph*, was "noted as a savage beast". But when the attack began, this dog raised no alarm; it failed to bark. The newspaper reported that it "lay perfectly still and quiet. So, it seems that the animal was familiar with one or other of the party."[79]

The raiders terrorised and severely injured Mr and Mrs Bradley and their servants and stole a large collection of silver items and over £100 in banknotes and gold. At the York Assizes, summing up after the trial, the judge said, "I have heard many cases of this kind, where robberies have been committed; but I am happy to say that this is the only case I have ever tried where such wanton, unnecessary, and barbarous cruelty was inflicted."

Some alleged members of the gang escaped prosecution owing to lack of evidence, but Daniel Dickinson, James Gleadhall, and Henry Marsden, accused of being the ringleaders, appeared in court. The proceedings were complicated and lengthy, but two points arose that illustrated the detectives' approach to this case.

First, Dickinson and three others were spotted, two days after the outrage, spending the evening drinking in a beer house, in a celebratory mood. Witnesses described them as having been "flush with money" and they were paying for their drinks with gold sovereigns – coins which they would not have received through their wage packets. The landlord, Benjamin Harrison, remarked on this to Dickinson, hinting that he wondered where this money had all come from. Dickinson replied – proud to deny that he had earned it by honest toil – "Only fools and horses work!" The Sheffield detectives also noted the significance of what appeared to be an open show of sudden wealth.[80]

Secondly, footprint evidence was produced by Inspectors Ephraim

Sills and Samuel Linley, who had hurried to the crime scene soon after the outrage occurred. In court, Inspector Linley stated that he arrived at *Manor Oaks* at eight o'clock on the morning of the attack. "On one of the flower beds in front of the house, I observed various footmarks – some as of India rubber overshoes, and others which were so peculiar that I thought it advisable to protect them from the weather by covering them with slates."

He then described this peculiar appearance: "It had eight rows of square nails; six of the rows were very distinct, and there was some irregularity in the position of the nails. One side appeared much higher than the other, leaving the two rows of nails on the other side almost invisible, as though the boots had been mended by a piece being put on the centre of the sole." [81]

The discovery and protection of these prints was observed and witnessed by one of Mr Bradley's servants, Joseph Linneker, and Mr Brailsford, a reporter from the *Independent*. Meantime, Inspector Sills had obtained James Gleadhall's boots, which Inspector Linley took to Manor Oaks where, comparing one of them with the footprint, he found that it "corresponded precisely".

The detectives and prosecutors would have been aware that doubts surrounded the validity of presenting footprints in court (because, even when matching boots or shoes, prints don't positively identify the wearer) but this carefully-gathered information was added to the collection of other evidence and it appears to have been unchallenged. [82]

※ ※ ※

During these mid-Victorian years, before fingerprints, photographs, and forensic science became available, defendants and their attorneys knew that the police were restricted when compiling evidence. So, they often confidently submitted "not guilty" pleas, assuming that they could not be disproved. But over-confident defendants who constructed false alibis, employed unreliable witnesses, or exaggerated their protests of innocence, risked losing all credibility: if one feature of their defence could be shown to be contrived, juries might infer that other features were similarly false.

At Sheffield Summer Sessions in 1858, at the end of a case that had lasted for seven hours, the chairman of the magistrates offered the jury an observation based on his experience over many years, that it was "a common practice in getting up cases of alibi, to make the circumstances of one day fit to another, so that in the case of a false alibi, the witnesses often spoke the truth as to everything, except the date." [83]

Criminals who felt that the local police were taking too much interest in their activities could be tempted to leave town and move on to another place, where they could shed their reputations for being "suspicious". But such plans often backfired because, in their new surroundings, runaway criminals risked becoming noticeable because they were strangers. During the nineteenth century, local accents were still quite distinctive, ignorance of local customs could attract attention, and even an unusual choice of clothes could be viewed with suspicion. Newcomers to a community could find it hard to disguise their roots. [84]

✳ ✳ ✳

In 1859, a pickpocketing incident occurred in Sheffield's cheese market. A newspaper report described this as having been committed by "one of the accomplished, well-dressed professionals" who had been noticed around the town during the past week. The theft wasn't discovered until a few minutes later, allowing the man time to disappear into the crowd. But his style of dress was noted and reported to the police. He then, unwisely, committed his next offence in the company of a fellow "professional" in the railway station booking office, within the full view of detectives Airey and Brayshaw.

When these men, William Johnson and Robert Owen, made their first appearance in court, they made the mistake of underestimating the Sheffield Police Force's efficiency. Acknowledging that they were strangers to the town, Johnson informed the magistrates that he lived in Vauxhall Street, Leeds, while Owen gave his address as 32 Princess Street, Stockport. Their second court appearance got off to a bad start: the Chief Constable informed the magistrates that there is no Vauxhall Street in Leeds, and that, though Stockport has a Princess Street, there is no number 32. [85]

A significant pickpocketing incident occurred, one evening in January 1862, when the Sheffield Literary and Philosophical Society held its monthly meeting at the Cutlers' Hall. [86] The Society had informed the Chief Constable beforehand, that a large audience was expected. Accordingly, two officers had been assigned to attend on crime-prevention duty: Detective Robert Airey and Sergeant John King took up positions overlooking the entrance hall and the front steps.

William Beale, the superintendent of Rotherham's Parkgate Iron Works, was in the audience. When the meeting had ended, as he was leaving through the crowded entrance hall, Mr. Beale felt a slight touch at his waistcoat pocket. Immediately, he discovered that his gold watch had been stolen. Suspicious of two men close to him, he pushed them into a corner and raised an alarm, detaining them until Detective Airey arrived. As Airey came running up the steps, he saw one of the men drop a gold watch on the floor. Airey picked it up, and showed it to Mr. Beale, who confirmed that it was his property. Sergeant King took the men, Edward Brown and James Hunter, into custody. Next day, in the magistrate's court, offering no defence, the men were committed for trial. [87]

Most local pickpockets could be recognised and named by Sheffield police officers. But Brown and Hunter were previously unknown – and this intrigued the detective team. In their view, this crime wasn't the work of novices: these two men were experienced; they must have been picking pockets before – but not in Sheffield. So, the Sheffield officers decided to extend their investigation. Over the two years since the Johnson and Owen case, technical developments had included an improvement in the accuracy and the availability of photography. So, although the equipment was still rather primitive, Brown and Hunter were photographed. The *Independent* reported that the photographs were taken "after a stout but fruitless resistance by the involuntary sitters". The photographer's persistence allowed the Sheffield police to send copies of these photographs to their colleagues in several surrounding towns. Positive replies were received from the police forces in Liverpool and Nottingham, where the two men were identified as criminals who had been convicted in those towns on several occasions, under various aliases. This example of sharing information formed an early step towards preventing criminals from using freedom to roam as a means of evading detection. [88]

An unusual case occurred in 1863. Messrs Hutton and Son, silver platers, with premises in the High Street, found that they had a problem. From time to time, money was going missing from a chest of drawers in the firm's counting house. Puzzled as to how these crimes were being carried out, the firm's owners sought help from the police, who found evidence that the drawers' locks had been "picked". The firm responded by changing the locks and strengthening the fronts of the drawers with brass plates. But still the robberies continued. Detective-Officer Brayshaw came to investigate and discovered that a piece of wood had been cut out of the back of the locked drawer, allowing access from behind. But still three important questions remained: Who was stealing the money, and exactly When? and How?

Suspicion fell on an errand boy, Henry Keeton. Officer Brayshaw searched him but found only a stolen cigar. When questioned about the cigar, however, Henry confessed to the thefts of money, and implicated three other boys.

The simplicity of their crime became apparent after studying the layout of the premises and discovering the staff's daily routine. The counting house and warehouse formed two halves of a single building. At one end was the counting-house's external door, while

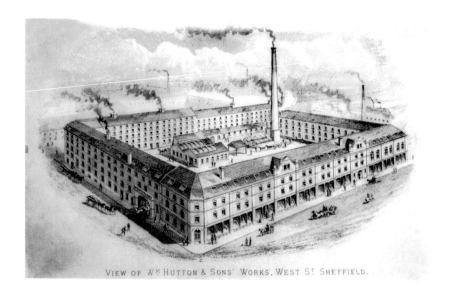

VIEW OF Wᴹ HUTTON & SONS' WORKS, WEST Sᵀ SHEFFIELD.

W. M Huttons & Sons

Few of Sheffield's firms that traded over a century ago remain in business today. But some manufacturers' former premises, despite redevelopment and war damage, have survived and are recognisable, though now occupied by more recent tenants. This factory was built for Huttons on West Street during the last years of the 19th century, to replace their High Street premises.

at the opposite end an external door led to and from the warehouse. But in the central wall that separated these departments, there was a communicating door.

Both the warehouse and counting house closed down during the firm's mid-day break, allowing staff to go for a meal. The counting house staff were in the habit of leaving via their own outer door, which they locked behind them; but responsibility for locking the warehouse door was usually left to one of these four boys. When they had an opportunity, the boys would leave the warehouse door unfastened. This allowed them to enter the building and slip through to the counting house where, while the clerks were away, one of the boys would raid the drawer and take the money, while the others kept watch.

The boys were all aged between eleven and fourteen – so, in view of the fact that they were dealing with minors, the magistrates ordered that their preliminary hearing should be suspended until further investigations had been carried out. They wished to eliminate the possibility that the boys' actions were being incited or in some way manipulated by an adult employee. Unfortunately for the boys and their families, no such connection was found. [89]

※　※　※

Some of the accused suspects who appeared in court seemed to reject the idea of planning a careful defence. Instead, however compelling the evidence against them, they would offer a stout denial, relying on fantasy rather than common sense.

※　※　※

One Wednesday night in January 1856, when Frederick Andrews closed his butcher's shop on Broad Lane, he felt sure that his locks and metal bars would, as usual, keep it secure against thieves. But the next morning, when he arrived to open up, Mr Andrews discovered that he had been burgled: the locks were broken, the bars had been levered off, and a large quantity of beef and mutton was missing. For the Sheffield police, this was just the latest of many recent shop robberies; detectives had already been questioning night watchmen about any suspicious persons they had seen in the neighbourhood. On this Thursday morning, one of the watchmen reported seeing a man loitering along Broad Lane on Wednesday night. When Detective Officer Charles Whaley was given this man's description, he was sure that it matched a character well known to him: Thomas Isles, a man with previous convictions for housebreaking, who lived in nearby Hawley Croft.

On the Thursday evening, between eight and nine o'clock, Detective Whaley, accompanied by Inspector Ephraim Sills, visited Thomas Isles' house. Isles was not at home, but in his kitchen the officers found a loin of beef and some joints of mutton, which they suspected of being part of the haul from Mr Andrews' shop. Also, in the oven, being cooked for supper, were another two large joints. Finding such a quantity of meat in this small house, the officers felt that their suspicions were well founded.

Inspector Sills carried the meat away to the police station, while Officer Whaley remained in the house, ready to apprehend Isles on his return home, and to prevent his wife from warning her husband that the police were waiting for him. There had still been no sign of Isles when Sills returned to Hawley Croft and took up a position on watch outside the house. But at a few minutes after midnight, Isles came up the street and entered his yard, where the inspector seized him. Isles had been walking with one hand in his jacket pocket. Sills pulled this hand out, finding that Isles was grasping a crowbar, eighteen inches long, with one end shaped as a curved chisel, and the other drawn out to a point – just the thing for wrenching off padlocks. In one of Isles' other pockets was found a "jemmy", and a bunch of five skeleton keys for picking door locks. One of these keys was the exact size required for unlocking Mr. Andrews' shop door.

Mr. Andrews was able to identify the meat found at Thomas Isles' house, as having been stolen from his shop. Most convincingly he recognised the back loin, because the beast's pelvis had been broken in a peculiar manner when the carcase was divided. Right and left halves were not symmetrical; instead, like two pieces of a jigsaw puzzle, their irregular edges fitted together precisely. This could not have been achieved if the two halves had come from different animals.

In court, Mr Andrews produced the loin from his shop (left behind by the burglar) and demonstrated how it locked in exactly to the half recovered from Isles's house. Still, Isles continued to claim that he had bought and paid for the meat, and had found the keys, crowbar and jemmy in a passage in West Bar Green, only five minutes before Inspector Sills apprehended him. The magistrates dismissed Isles's account and committed him for trial at the next assizes. [90]

Footnotes

73. 1858, SDT, 1 June; SI, 31 July.
74. William Thompson *(1811 – 80)* was the youngest of triplet brothers born in Nottingham. Their mother informally gave her triplets middle names to celebrate Shadrack, Meshack and Abednego, described in the Old Testament book *Daniel*, as the heroes who confronted and defeated Nebuchadnezzer, the King of Babylon. When he reached his teenage years, William "Abednego" Thompson developed a talent for prize fighting, and used his middle name, simplified to "Bendigo", to publicise a very successful career. He won the all-England championship in 1839 and held this title until he retired undefeated in 1850. His memory is honoured in Nottingham in various ways. (For example, the city's tram No. 203 carries the name William "Bendigo" Thompson.)
   For more biographical information, see https://nottinghamhiddenhistoryteam.wordpress.com/2016/02/09/william-bendigo-thompson/
75. 1861: SDT, 28 and 29 October; 1880: Sporting Life, 25 August.
76. 1865: SI, 4, 6, 14, 22 and 25 February; SDT, 6, 11, 18 February.
77. 1859: SDN, 21 October; SDT, 21 October; SI, 22 October; and 1867: SDT & SI, 4 July.
78. 1858: SDT, 21, 23 January, 3 February, 12 March, and 27 April; SI, 23 January, 6, 9, 13 February, and 13 March.
79. This may have been true. Newspaper reports mention that the raiders appeared to be familiar with the layout of the building, they addressed Mr Bradley by name, and they had all taken the precaution of wearing masks.
   In Conan Doyle's short story, *Silver Blaze*, first published in the *Strand* magazine in December 1892 (thirty-six years after the *Manor Oaks* outrage), identification of the horse as the killer of its trainer John Straker, owes much to Sherlock Holmes's famous observation (in recent years borrowed as the title of a popular book and film). Holmes's cryptic response – as a tutor to his pupil, when Inspector Gregory

begs for elucidation – is to point out "The curious incident of the dog in the night-time". This curious incident was that guard dog at the stable did not bark – indicating that the overnight visitor wasn't a stranger but a familiar person: in fact, the horse's trainer.

80. The detectives may have drawn on this experience, two years later, to aid identification of the four men who fled to Sheffield after stealing money by committing a garotte robbery in Leeds.

81. In his short story, *The Beryl Coronet*, first published in 1892, Conan Doyle sets an ideal scene for Holmes to impress readers with his skill at interpreting footprints. Holmes and Watson had travelled to the home of a rich banker, Alexander Holder, where there had been a robbery – and a recent snowfall. Holmes interviewed Mary, Holder's niece, who confirmed that their housemaid, Lucy Parr, had a boyfriend, Francis Prosper. Having examined the path that ran alongside the house, Holmes startled Miss Holder by calmly remarking (though he had never met this young man) that Francis has a wooden leg. *"Why, you are like a magician!" said she. "How do you know that?"* Holmes just smiled and left her wondering. Understandably, Conan Doyle didn't wish to complicate his plot by getting tied up in discussions about rows of nails – and, in any case, he wouldn't be required to convince a judge and jury. Instead, he settled for a trail of small, round prod marks.

82. 1856: SDT, December 10, 12, 26, 27; SI, December 20, 27. 1857: SI, January 3, 13, and March 7, 21 (2 items); SDT, January 14.

83. 1858: SI, August 28.

84. A criminal's relocation brought mixed blessings for the police: one force's relief at losing an old troublemaker could simply become another force's problem of recognising a new troublemaker.

85. 1859: SDN, November 30, and December 3; SDT. December 3.
The exposure of Johnson and Owen's deceit illustrates the Sheffield force's efficiency and attention to detail. A check on these men's addresses would probably have required telegraphic communication with their colleagues in Leeds and Stockport.

86. Sheffield's Literary and Philosophical Society (the "Lit and Phil") met monthly from 1822 through to 1932, holding lectures and demonstrations to keep its members in touch with a wide range of topics: archaeology, natural history, the physical and chemical sciences, as well as subjects more obviously assumed within its title.

For more information, see http://collections.museums-sheffield.org.uk/view/
people/asitem/items@null:2434/0?t:state:flow=8768f4f5-382d-4ddb-bd0d-
9329a5733187

87. 1862: SDT, January 18, 30; SI, January 29, 30.

88. 1862: SI, March 8.

The photographer faced the challenge of preventing these men from moving while
the photographs were being taken. Movement during the exposure would have
blurred the images, robbing them of any value. In 1862, photographic materials (glass
plates, not film) were relatively unresponsive: exposure times lasting 3 or 4 seconds
would have been needed for forming satisfactory images. Customers who visited
a studio to have a portrait taken would have been grateful for the photographer's
use of a device to support the back of the head, to keep it perfectly still and allow
photographs to be sharp. But unco-operative "sitters", such as Hunter and Brown,
would have deliberately shaken their heads, blinked their eyes and moved their lips,
to frustrate the photographer's (and the detectives') hope of success.

Over the next few years, photographic materials improved – they became "faster"
– so that exposure times could be safely shortened. This situation would have been
reached, eight years later, when the *Sheffield Daily Telegraph* published a short
news item under the heading *Pleasant Prospects for Photographers*: "With the view
to the more complete identification of habitual criminals, the Home Secretary
asks that the police should be furnished with photographic likenesses of all those
offenders at present in prison, and it was mentioned at a meeting of the Middlesex
magistrates that 10,000 photographs would be required every year." (1870, SDT,
February 26)

89. 1863, SI, April 25, and May 2.

90. 1856: SI, January 19; SDT, January 19, and March 5.

Wortley Hall

The isolated setting of this impressive building, the country seat
of the Wharncliffe Barons and Earls, acted as a magnet for burglars,
including the occasion in 1859, when a house guest was deprived of
his money and possessions – but only for a short time,
until Sheffield's detectives had solved the case.

CHAPTER SEVEN

APPRECIATION AND HARDSHIP

During August 1859, Lord Wharncliffe and his wife hosted a shooting party at their country mansion, Wortley Hall. The guests, numbering around 70, included one of their military friends, The Hon. Major Frazer, who was allocated a bedroom on the ground floor. Late one evening, when he retired to rest, the weather being hot and sultry, Major Frazer decided to leave the window open overnight. Next morning, he woke to discover that a burglar had stolen some of his property: a pair of trousers, a pair of patent leather boots, an expensive dressing gown, a pair of cuff links and several other gold accessories, a pair of razors, and a £20 note had gone missing.

Major Frazer checked the facts with his valet and was about to report the crime to the local constable of the West Riding Police Force, when Lord Wharncliffe intervened and insisted on taking alternative action.[91] The *Sheffield Independent* reported that his Lordship, "having more confidence in the practised skill of the Sheffield detectives, contacted Mr. Jackson, the Chief Constable and, having consulted with him, gave full information to Detective Officer Brayshaw, with instructions to announce a reward of £20 and to take such further steps as he might deem necessary to enable him to capture the thief."

Detective Brayshaw's search took him on a complicated route, taking in both the Wortley area and the Sheffield town centre. Picking up clues as he went, he interviewed people who had seen the thief, identified as Joseph Worrell, eventually finding him at a beer house in Howbrook. Worrell was taken to the police station in Sheffield, and within two days, he appeared in court, charged with committing burglary and theft.

Worrell's behaviour had contributed to his capture: he had made no secret of his sudden wealth. He had offered the £20 note (a huge sum in 1859) when buying a drink, he had retained the distinctive gold items on his person and had been wearing Major Frazer's trousers and boots. The boots were quite distinctive: one had a heel higher than the other – a compensation for the major's having broken his thigh, some years ago.

In court, Worrell said he knew nothing about the burglary and he denied all charges, claiming that the gold items were his – he'd "had them for years". When questioned about the boots, he said that they had been specially altered for him because he had an ulcer on his heel.

He was remanded in custody and later appeared at the York Assizes. [92]

Sheffield's factories and warehouses were regularly targeted by burglars, but retail shops suffered too – especially the town's jewellers and watchmakers.

The following year, a robbery took place at the King Street premises of the jewellers, Messrs. G. and J.C. Burrell. This crime provided the detectives with an unusually complicated challenge, demanding much time, effort, and patience. The robbers were two brothers, Thomas and James McCabe, who sought to protect themselves against conviction by using an intricate plan of deception. Eventually, however, they were brought to justice.

Messrs. Burrell expressed their gratitude for the police force's hard work in a letter to the Chairman of the Watch Committee, which summarises this case so clearly that it can be quoted exactly as written.

Sir,—You may perhaps recollect that in March last year we suffered a most audacious robbery of three valuable gold watches from our shop – the thief getting clear off with his booty; that the man who was charged with the robbery was acquitted of that charge at the York Assizes in July, and no clue of the property could then be discovered; that nearly seven months after the robbery, when all reasonable hope of recovering the property had expired, your Detective officers Airey and Brayshaw, in the most ingenious manner, without any aid from us, and, indeed without our knowledge, traced the property to three different pawnbrokers' shops – two at Rotherham and one at Sheffield – where it had been pledged by the brother of the man who was charged with the robbery; that these officers, then, and in the most skilful and energetic manner, got a clue to the man who had pledged the watches, whom they traced from Sheffield to London, from London to Southampton, and thence to St Helier, in the island of Jersey; that there Brayshaw captured his man and brought him to Sheffield; and that the prisoner was tried at the last York Assizes, convicted, and sentenced, and the whole of our valuable property restored to us.

Thus, when we had utterly given up the hope of recovering our goods, and the guilty parties had entirely eluded justice, the matter, after the lapse of so many months, seemed beyond all reasonable doubt to end there. But through the vigilance of your officers, Airey and Brayshaw, the guilty were punished, and our goods were recovered; and knowing more of the way in which these results were accomplished than we can now explain we cannot speak in any measured terms of admiration of the persevering skill of these two able and valuable officers, nor can we permit the opportunity to slip, without expressing in some more tangible shape our desire to encourage them in the continued exercise of their skill for the safety and benefit of the public.

We have, therefore, to ask your committee kindly to permit us to present Airey and Brayshaw each with a good silver watch, bearing any inscription which your committee or the Chief Constable may suggest. We wish to do this simply from a sense of gratitude to the officers, and of our duty to the public. We know that society has a right to expect that every member of your force will do his duty, but it is possible, as this instance clearly proves, for a man to do even more than his duty, better than well, and thus to merit the utmost encouragement from the public. We believe that two such able officers as Airey and Brayshaw are an invaluable acquisition both to the town and your force; and seeing how much the safety of society depends upon the efficiency of the police, we earnestly hope that the deserts of these two valuable officers will be more generally recognised, and that no effort way be spared to retain them in your force.

We do not wish this letter or the subject to be made public, unless your committee think it would do the officers any service. We should have preferred to do as we propose privately, but find the law compels us to take this step first. [93]

The writer's last point – about "the law" – referred to the Watch Committee's *Rules, Orders and Regulations*, which clearly set out its policy on preventing bribery and corruption. They state that, as a condition of a police officer's appointment, "He shall not on any pretence whatever receive money by way of donation or gratuity, directly or indirectly, for anything done in the execution of his duty, without the express consent or permission in writing of the Watch Committee."

※ ※ ※

On Saturday morning, 10 November 1860, headlines in Sheffield's newspapers announced a "Great Jewellery Robbery" (*Independent*) and "Extensive Robbery of Jewellery and Watches Last Night" (*Daily Telegraph*).

Last night, between eleven and twelve o'clock, the shop of Mr. Benjamin Cohen, jeweller, 27, High Street, was broken into and a large number of watches, gold chains and other articles stolen from the window. Mr. Cohen sleeps on the premises, but after closing his shop last night at about a quarter past eleven, he left by the back door, locking it behind him, intending to be absent a very short time.

At a quarter past twelve o'clock, Mr. Cohen returned and, to his dismay, found the back door open. When he entered the shop, he saw at once that a great number of watches and chains had been removed. Mr. Cohen ran into the street, found a policeman and told him of his loss, which was then reported to the Town Hall. Detectives James Winn and William Leonard went immediately to Mr Cohen's shop to assess the damage. They found that in their haste to get away, the thieves had only taken goods from shop window; they had left gold in the till and a drawer full of valuable diamond rings and watches untouched.

About two hours later, when the second editions were published, these reports had been hastily extended; extra headlines read "Capture of the Thieves and the Whole of the Stolen Property" (*Independent*) and "Apprehension of the Thieves and Recovery of the Stolen Property" (*Telegraph*).

About 4 o'clock this morning, shortly after starting to print this edition, we were glad to learn through the Chief Constable, that two men have been apprehended by Detective-Officers Airey and Brayshaw, with the whole of the property in their possession. [94]

The background to these amazingly quick arrests was revealed about six weeks later, when the two thieves, Joseph Hawley and Thomas Hayes, appeared at the York Assizes.

For some time, Detective-officers Airey and Brayshaw had had their eye on these two men: they had observed them lurking about in the neighbourhood of Mr. Cohen's shop on several nights before the robbery took place and had found out that they lived in Duke Street. So, on being informed about the robbery, the detectives made their way to Duke Street, where they concealed themselves. At about one o'clock, the men came up the street and were captured.

A skeleton key was found on one of the men, and an ordinary house-door key on the other. After taking the men to the Town Hall, where they were held, the detectives went to the house where the mother of one of the men lived – only about 100 yards from where the men were captured. The house key they had found fitted the door, so the officers went in, where they found a bag containing a number of gold watches tied up in a handkerchief, and a quantity of gold chains, pins, and wedding rings. Later, these goods were identified by Mr. Cohen as his property, and the detectives were able to confirm their suspicion that the skeleton key they had found fitted Mr. Cohen's kitchen door. [95]

Detectives Brayshaw and Airey had been off-duty when the burglary was committed, but they responded immediately when told about it. In view of their recent observations, they strongly suspected that Hawley and Hayes were the men responsible. They also anticipated that the stolen goods would not be found where the men lived: these were professional criminals, who knew better than to hide stolen goods in their bedrooms. Instead, the detectives expected them to have chosen somewhere close by – such as in the house where Hayes' mother lived.

The detectives' astute action raised the Sheffield Police Force's reputation; but it also unexpectedly triggered a debate that challenged the Watch Committee's much-valued philosophy concerning crime prevention.

Within a week of the thieves' capture, the following news appeared in the *Daily Telegraph*:

We are glad to announce that a subscription is on foot for the purpose of presenting a suitable reward to Detective Officers Airey and Brayshaw for the intelligence and activity displayed by them in the capture of the whole of the property stolen from the shop of Mr Cohen, jeweller. It is worthy of remark that the property, worth between £500 and £600, was traced and recovered without any material damage having been sustained by it. [96]

Similar coverage of this affair appeared in the *Independent*, which added:

We understand Mr. Cohen has offered a subscription of £5. If recovery of the property had been delayed a few hours, Mr Cohen would probably have offered a reward of £50 or £100. We have no doubt the Watch Committee will testify their appreciation of the services of the two officers with prompt liberality. [97]

Many owners of town-centre businesses supported the appeal, to reward the police force and encourage them to maintain their surveillance; but also, to warn criminals contemplating further burglaries that they would be wise stay away.

Members of the Police Force Sub-Committee might have regretted that this crime had not been *prevented*, but they evidently approved of the detectives' work. At their meeting on November 22, they agreed upon a proposal for submission to the Town Council, that Richard Brayshaw and Robert Airey should both be promoted to the rank of Merit Class detectives and that their wages should be raised by three shillings a week.

When this recommendation was discussed in the council chamber, however, some councillors opposed it, raising objections based on their own interpretations of the Watch Committee's principle of crime *prevention*.

Alderman Francis Hoole (a former Mayor) rose to ask whether the officers who apprehended the burglars in Mr Cohen's case were the same who had observed the men lounging about for a fortnight previously. If they were, he should like to know why those men were entitled to the thanks of the Watch Committee or the Council. When the officers saw these men lounging about, it was their duty to have apprehended them and taken them to the Town Hall. The detectives would have been perfectly justified in apprehending the men who committed the robbery, as rogues and vagabonds.

Councillor Charles Alcock supported him. He said that if the police were aware of the presence of suspicious characters in the town, and could have taken steps to prevent the robbery, but did not do so, it was a queer arrangement that they should receive a payment.

But other councillors drew attention to the principle of civil liberty. Alderman Thomas Mycock said he was surprised to hear Alderman Hoole's remarks, because no man could be seized and taken before a magistrate without sufficient cause. He pointed out that if Detectives Brayshaw and Airey had arrested Hawley and Hayes before a crime had been committed, they would have been liable to an action for false imprisonment. Alderman Mycock was supported by other councillors, and when a vote was taken, the Watch Committee's recommendations were approved by a sizeable majority. [98]

When the proceedings of the Town Council became known, it was the newspapers' turn to pass comment. An editorial in the *Independent* denounced the opinion voiced by Alderman Hoole:

Statements to the effect that Airey and Brayshaw knew of the robbery beforehand and ought to have prevented it are simply monstrous. Airey and Brayshaw had no doubt reason to believe that a serious robbery was likely to be committed somewhere in the town, and, like prudent and skilful officers, they made themselves fully acquainted with the places of rendezvous of the suspected parties. They no sooner learned that Mr

Cohen had been robbed than they used that knowledge with such effect
as not only to capture the thieves, but to recover the whole of the booty.
A capture more skilfully managed, or more creditable in every respect to
the officers has not been made in Sheffield for many years; and we are
glad that the meritorious conduct of Airey and Brayshaw has not been
allowed to pass without recognition. [99]

The town councillors who heavily criticised police strategy failed to
appreciate the hardships that police officers had to endure. Visible
injuries sustained while quelling violence could receive immediate
treatment from the police surgeon and possibly a little sympathy;
but the health hazards suffered by officers who spent long hours on
foot patrol, in all weathers, was a different matter: some diseases
developed so gradually that they could become serious before they
became obvious. Because working conditions were so harsh, there was
a high drop-out rate among newly-recruited constables. Officers who
persisted with their work earned the satisfaction of achievement – "a
job well done" – but at a price: bronchitis, arthritis, rheumatism, and
pneumonia brought many careers to a premature end. These effects
were not confined to the lower ranks. In those days, promotion to the
rank of sergeant or inspector did not provide a path to a "desk job". The
officers selected for these higher positions had to set an example – and
this inevitably meant continued practical duty and exposure to risk.

Significant changes occurred within the Sheffield Police Force team of
detectives during the period 1862 – 67, following the deaths of Ephraim
Sills, Robert Airey, and Richard Brayshaw. These three events were
similar in many unfortunate respects.

- Death, judged in each case to be premature, resulted from long-
standing disease brought on by occupational strains and hazards.
- All the men died at home, each leaving a widow and a young

family, at a time when superannuation support for widows was only modest and of short duration.

- In the hope of easing their financial hardships, public collections were organised for each widow and her family, in turn, and newspaper editorials urged the Watch Committee to be generous and sensitive to the needs of the bereaved.

- Their funerals were attended by civic leaders, with a full and formal turnout of the police force, showing sincere respect for their former colleagues' achievements and sacrifices. Their funeral processions through the streets were witnessed and accompanied by large crowds.

- Each death, in turn, was marked in the newspapers by an obituary and a substantial report of the funeral ceremony. *(Some extracts now follow.)*

Detective Inspector Ephraim Sills died on 7 March 1862, of consumption, aged 40. He left a widow and seven young children. The funeral was held at the Church of St John the Evangelist, Hyde Park – where Inspector Sills' body was interred.

Ephraim Sills, the senior member of the team, came from a police family (his father was a village constable in north Nottinghamshire). He had served in the Sheffield force for about 15 years and was widely known among members of the public. Prompt and vigilant in his duties, he was much respected by all who had his acquaintance. He would be remembered as an active man of shrewd judgement, with a remarkable memory. [100]

Detective Inspector Robert Airey died on 13 November 1865, of consumption, aged 36. He left a widow and seven young children. He had been a policeman for about sixteen years: for the past nine years as a detective, and for the past three (since the death of Ephraim Sills) as the Inspector leading the detective team.

He merited and received the esteem of his fellows, and the confidence and support of his superiors and the public – among whom he was universally known. Upright and able, he was conscientious in the discharge of his duty, gentlemanly in his demeanour, and respectful to all. He tracked the burglar, the murderer, the garrotter, the lawless of all classes, often through the dark hours of the night, amidst rain and snow. No offence of any importance was committed in which Robert Airey was not successfully engaged, but in recent years he had worked while in a declining state of health. Intermittent rest periods allowed him to rally but the disease returned with redoubled violence, and, after a month's confinement at home, he quietly passed away. [101]

Detective Officer Richard Brayshaw died on 24 February 1867, aged 40, leaving a widow and nine young children. He had served in the Sheffield Police Force for sixteen years, including 10 years as a detective officer.

The cause of his death was consumption, of rather long standing, acquired during the discharge of his professional duties which brought him, often in conjunction with Detective Airey, a very much deserved reputation. Working as a team, achieving success in their ingenious and enterprising undertakings, Airey and Brayshaw's qualities so fully complemented each other that between them they displayed every quality a good detective could ever need.

Brayshaw's leading characteristic, so odd in a detective, was that he "would speak his mind if he died for it". His directness and intrepidity of action were at times astonishing. Though himself lacking size, he would, when entrusted with the task of apprehending a notorious and powerful criminal, approach his prisoner, and capture him as though it was the most natural thing in the world, and resistance was out of the question. He displayed fearless courage in every emergency.

But for two or three years past, weakened by the insidious advances of his malady, he was at intervals extremely ill and has several times been sent away by the Chief Constable in the hope that a change of air might restore him to health.

Recently, however, he was confined to his bed, lingering on between life and death, until he finally succumbed.[102]

It was sixteen years since he had left Harewood.

Footnotes

91. Until 1974, when the county of South Yorkshire was created, Sheffield lay within the historic West Riding of Yorkshire. Although the West Riding Constabulary covered the whole of the West Riding, its responsibilities tended to concentrate on the rural villages and townships, because larger centres of population such as Sheffield were served mainly by their own forces. Both the Sheffield and West Riding forces were proud of their reputations, and if rivalry arose between them, it always appeared to be professional and respectful. On some occasions, they co-operated in investigating a crime, the outrage at Cawthorne being an example. But at Wortley Hall, Lord Wharncliffe was in a privileged position, allowing him to dictate who should solve his criminal problems.

For more information, see http://british-police-history.uk/show_nav. cgi?force=west_riding&tab=0&page=west_riding&nav=alpha

92. 1859: SDA, August 5 and 10, November 26, December 8; SI, August 6 and13, December 10; SDT, August 6, 10, and December 8; Leeds Mercury, August 6 and 11; Morning Post, August 8; Derbyshire Times, December 10.

93. 1861, SDT, March 26, April 1, September 21, October 10, 12, and December 7, 14; SI, March 30, October 10, 12, November 1,

94. 1860, SDT, November 10; SI, November 10.

95. 1860, SDT, December 21; SI, December 22.

96. 1860, SDT, November 17.

97. 1860, SI, November 17.

98. 1860, SDT, December 13

99. 1861, SI, January 19; SDT, January 14.

100. 1862, SDT, March 8, 11; April 16; SI, March 11, 15; April 16.

101. 1865, SDT, November 18.

102. 1867, SDT, February 28; March 1, 2, 5, 11, 14, 15, 16; SI, March 2.

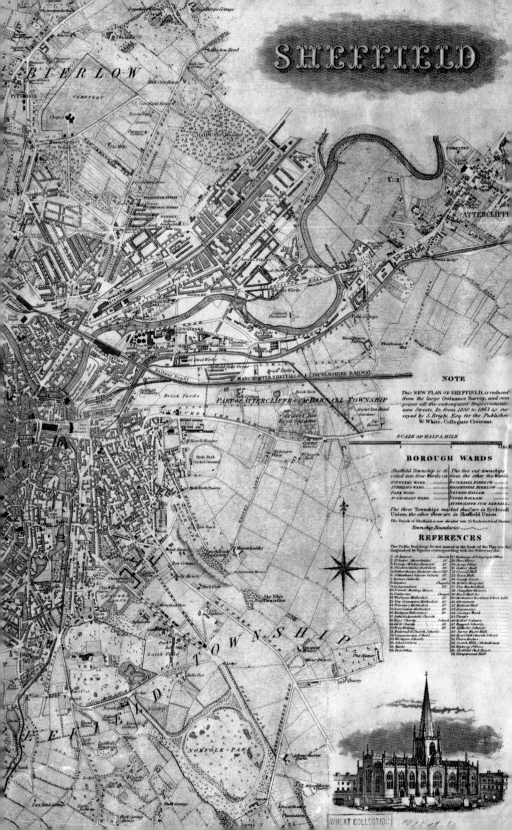

SHEFFIELD

BIERLOW

ATTERCLIFFE

MANCHESTER SHEFFIELD & LINCOLNSHIRE RAILWAY

PART OF ATTERCLIFFE CUM DARNALL TOWNSHIP

ECCLESALL TOWNSHIP

NORFOLK PARK

NOTE

This NEW PLAN OF SHEFFIELD, is reduced from the large Ordnance Survey, and comprises all the subsequent Improvements, new Streets, &c. from 1850 to 1863 as surveyed by J. Brigly, Esq. for the Publisher W. White, Collegiate Crescent.

SCALE OF HALF A MILE

BOROUGH WARDS

Sheffield Township is divided into four Wards; viz.	The five out townships form the other five Wards
STPETERS WARD	ECCLESALL BIERLOW
STPHILIPS WARD	BRIGHTSIDE BIERLOW
PARK WARD	NETHER HALLAM
STGEORGES WARD	UPPER HALLAM
	ATTERCLIFFE CUM DARNALL

The three Townships marked thus⋆are in Ecclesall Union; the other three are in Sheffield Union.

The Parish of Sheffield is now divided into 25 Ecclesiastical Districts.

Township Boundaries ....

REFERENCES

The Public Buildings &c. not named in the Body of the Plan, are distinguished by figures corresponding with the following list.

1. St James........................Church
2. St Andrews (Bossville)............D[o]
3. Trinity (Wicker District).........D[o]
4. St Johns (Park District).........D[o]
5. St Matthew (Carver Street)......D[o]
6. Roman Catholic..................D[o]
7. Baptist..........................Chapel
8. Independent.....................D[o]
9. Friends Meeting House............D[o]
10. Unitarian.......................Chapel
11. Independent....................D[o]
12. New Connexion Methodist........D[o]
13. Primitive Methodist.............D[o]
14. Association Methodist..........D[o]
15. Wesleyan Methodist.............D[o]
16. Wesleyan Reformers..............D[o]
17. Catholic Apostolic Church.......D[o]
18. Boys' Charity................School
19. Free Writing..................D[o]
20. National & Church Schools.....D[o]
21. Lancasterian School...........D[o]
22. Wesleyan Schools..............D[o]
23. School of Arts...............D[o]
24. Post Office
25. Banks
26. Post Office

27. Exchange & Telegraph Office
28. Fire Offices
29. Assay Office
30. Cutlers' Hall
31. Council Hall
32. Town Hall
33. Town Hall
34. County Court
35. Public Hospital
36. New Market Hall
37. Old Market Hall
38. Slaughter Houses
39. Music Hall &c
40. Mechanics Institute & New Library
41. Athenaeum
42. Medical Hall
43. Dispensary
44. Savings Bank
45. Theatre
46. Public Baths
47. Ragged Schools
48. Gas &c Schools
49. Surrey Music Hall
50. Brunswick Church School
51. Union Rooms
52. Girls Club (St Andrews)
53. Railway Offices
54. Sheffield Club House
55. Temperance Hall

WHEAT COLLECTION

ACKNOWLEDGEMENTS

This book could not have been written without the encouragement and assistance I received from relatives and friends. Crucially, I must thank my cousin, Hazel Goodwin, for bringing the Brayshaw family of Harewood to my attention. As my investigation widened to include the families of Richard Brayshaw's detective colleagues, I was aided by some of their present-day descendants. In Lancashire, Alan Fiddling and his sister, Stella, shared some memories of earlier generations of the Airey family. In Yorkshire, Sandra Carnall introduced me to her uncle, George Carnall, brother-in-law of the late John Brayshaw Airey (a great-grandson of both Richard Brayshaw and Robert Airey). It was George who urged me to develop a modest account of the Brayshaw family's history into a version that might appeal to a wider readership.

In common with most Sheffield writers, I have very much valued the facilities provided by the city's Libraries and Archives. When the draft manuscript was ready to be examined by fresh pairs of eyes, many friends and neighbours were willing to take this task on, spotting weaknesses and offering suggestions which led to improvements in the text. I am grateful to them all. I would also like to thank Valerie Bayliss, chair of the Friends of the Old Town Hall.

Transformation of a pile of A4 sheets plus attached notes, etc., into a recognisable book requires professional expertise. I am very fortunate to have received this specialised service from my son, Nic Carter, and his wife, Myfanwy. I thank them heartily and sincerely.

But above all, I must acknowledge the debt I owe to my wife, Sheila, whose customary patience and good humour have been put to the test so many times during the past two years, when our domestic calm has been disturbed by a writer's eccentricity.